More Praise for the First Edition of *Make Your Contacts Count*

"A must-read for anyone who wants to get a job or make a career change."
> —Lisa Keathley, Career Development Center Director, School of Foreign Service, Georgetown University School of Foreign Service

"This book is the first tool I recommend to the people I coach."
> —Linda Marks, Corning, Inc.

"Baber & Waymon show how to connect for the right reasons, ones that make others feel important and valued, rather than used."
> —Bruce Nolan, Director, Treasury Executive Institute, U.S. Government

"One of the top books ever produced on the subject."
> —Dinah Adkins, National Business Incubation Association

"Essential knowledge for any professional or businessperson."
> —Jack Cole, Ph.D., The Johns Hopkins University

"A must-read to gain the competitive edge."
> —Anne Kelly, CEO, Federal Consulting Group

"As the world becomes flatter, our relationships become even more important. Unless you live in a cave, insolated from the world, you need this book."
> —Ane Powers, The White Hawk Group, LLC

Make Your Contacts Count

Networking Know-How for Business and Career Success

Second Edition

Anne Baber

Lynne Waymon

American Management Association

New York • Atlanta • Brussels • Chicago • Mexico City • San Francisco
Shanghai • Tokyo • Toronto • Washington, D.C.

Special discounts on bulk quantities of AMACOM books are available to corporations, professional associations, and other organizations. For details, contact Special Sales Department, AMACOM, a division of American Management Association, 1601 Broadway, New York, NY 10019.
Tel: 800-250-5308. Fax: 518-891-2372.
E-mail: specialsls@amanet.org
Website: www. amacombooks.org/go/specialsales
To view all AMACOM titles go to: www.amacombooks.org

This publication is designed to provide accurate and authoritative information in regard to the subject matter covered. It is sold with the understanding that the publisher is not engaged in rendering legal, accounting, or other professional service. If legal advice or other expert assistance is required, the services of a competent professional person should be sought.

Library of Congress Cataloging-in-Publication Data

Baber, Anne
    Make your contacts count : networking know-how for business and career success / Anne Baber and Lynne Waymon.—2nd ed.
        p.   cm.
    Includes index.
    ISBN-13: 978-0-8144-7402-0
    ISBN-10: 0-8144-7402-0
    1. Career development.   2. Business networks.   3. Social networks.
    4. Interpersonal relations.   5. Business etiquette.   6. Success in business.
    I. Waymon, Lynne.   II. Title.

    HF5381.B143   2007
    650.1'3—dc22   2006031977

Printing number

10   9

Contents

Preface

Get Ready for State-of-the-Art Networking

Everybody has contacts. Not everybody has contacts that count. How about you?

As we've researched, written about, and spoken on networking, we've discovered that only a fraction of people intuitively know how to network. Everybody else can—and must—learn how.

The Time Is Right

When we began researching our first book in 1987, networking had its niche as a job-hunting and career advancement tool. And women, wanting to break through the glass ceiling, saw how men in business helped each other and called it "the old-boys' network." Women's networking groups were springing up to encourage women to learn the skills and to help each other. Networking was seen as an extracurricular activity, not one sanctioned by or encouraged by employers unless, of course, it was for sales or business development.

Things have changed since then. In the last several years, networking—often under a pseudonym—has become a hot topic. Professors in business schools, senior executives in government, and heads of corporations all tout relationship building as the key to success.

You can hardly pick up a business school journal without seeing an article on networking. University research is exploring such topics as "social capital," "communities of practice," and "horizontal integration."

One of the competencies now required for entry into the Senior Executive Service—the U.S. government's top ranking jobs—is Building Coalitions/Communications. That competency is defined as the ability to explain, advocate, and express facts and ideas in a convincing manner and to negotiate with individuals and groups internally and externally. That competency also requires the ability to develop an expansive professional network with other organizations and to identify the internal and external politics that impact the work of the organization.

Corporate leaders are now seeing the business value of relationship building. The CEO of one Fortune 500 company recently announced an initiative with five elements. Four of those imperatives can only be accomplished as employees become proficient in the concepts and skills we cover in this book. What could be a louder call or clearer definition for networking than this imperative: "Establish enduring, inclusive relationships within (the company) and with our customers, employees, teammates, and community. Enable mutually beneficial partnerships that take full advantage of internal and external synergies. Understand the impact of personal behavior on others, and place a high priority on honesty and integrity."

So, just why is networking so important in today's business environment?

▶Networking is now *the essential professional competency* for employees at all levels. They need to develop strategic networking skills and practices to excel at creating, cultivating, and capitalizing on the cross-functional relationships that get things done and affect the bottom line.

▶Networking is now *the most important tool* for intelligence gathering. In business settings, such as conferences, trade shows, meetings, and even golf outings, people need leading-edge networking skills to find the latest information on resources, trends, and best practices.

▶Networking is now *the antidote* to the coming brain drain as baby boomers retire. Experienced employees need networking expertise so they can pass on their valuable organizational and technical knowledge to newer, younger staff members.

▶Networking is now *the critical strategy* for business development. Professionals and entrepreneurs need to know how to gain visibility and credibility in their target markets, and how to build and maintain relationships for long-term growth.

▶Networking is now *a must-have capability* for professional association members. Members need networking skills to take advantage of great connections at professional association meetings and conferences and to bring back new ideas and practices into their places of business.

▶Networking is *the know-how* for doing business in the U.S. International businesspeople and students need to get comfortable with and competent in the cultural ground rules for building relationships with Americans.

▶Networking is *the method* for personnel retention because it creates feelings of inclusion and helps people from diverse backgrounds feel listened to and valued at work.

▶Networking remains *the primary technique* that people use to find new jobs, change careers, or land on their feet after a layoff, merger, or reorganization. People who are looking for career advancement need practical networking strategies to become the natural and only choice in the job market.

Are You Ready?

As you go through life, from graduation to the grave, you'll have thousands of encounters with people in business and social settings.

▶You know that networking is important. Yet, you may wonder exactly how to create, cultivate, and capitalize on networking relationships and opportunities.

▶You know you should get networking on your calendar. Yet, you may have trouble trying to fit it into your busy lifestyle.

▶You know you need other people's help to get your projects, ideas, and initiatives off the ground. Yet, you may be unsure about how to connect with key people to get the job done.

▶You know that visibility often results in promotability. Yet, you may feel uncomfortable and shy about how to raise your profile in a way that fits your organizational culture.

▶You know that networking is the way to expand your customer/ client list. Yet, you may wish you knew more about planning networking Projects that give you top of the mind awareness with clients and referral sources.

▶You know you should join groups to network. Yet, you may be unclear about how to select the best ones and how to use them to advance your career and business goals.

▶You know it's valuable to go to professional meetings, trade shows, and conferences. Yet, you may wish you were better equipped to uncover resources, opportunities, and best practices at these venues.

▶You know that your executives are pushing teamwork, connectivity, horizontal integration, social capital, and the idea that business development is everybody's job. Yet, you may need to sharpen your interpersonal skills to be a player.

That's why we wrote this book: So that you can make networking an art . . . not an accident.

The Contacts Count Networking System

This book, the second edition of our fifth book, presents, for the first time in print, The Contacts Count Networking System (see Figure P-1). Here, you will find step-by-step guides to all aspects of networking. Most important, our System will help you take your networking from scattershot to streamlined and strategic.

Part I of this book gives you the tools to Survey Your Skills and Mindset. Measuring your mastery of various networking skills will give you a baseline. As you complete the comprehensive fifty-

FIGURE P-1. The Contacts Count System.

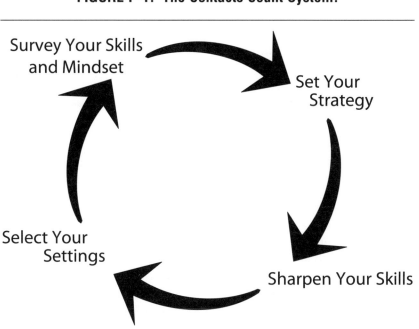

Survey Your Skills and Mindset

Set Your Strategy

Select Your Settings

Sharpen Your Skills

question Self-Assessment, you'll be able to see which skills are solidly part of your repertoire, and which ones you'll need to work on. But your skill level is only one part of your starting base. It also makes sense for you to become more conscious of the beliefs you hold about networking so that you're not held back by misconceptions or outdated attitudes.

Part II provides the underlying networking concepts you'll need to Set Your Strategy. After you know where you stand, you're ready for some big-picture concepts. We believe that the key to building relationships is trust. The Trust Matrix portrays the power of demonstrating your Character and Competence with everyone you meet. Once you understand how trust is created, you'll want to see what kinds of relationships are possible as you network. The Six-Stages Model provides a realistic picture of the variety of relationships that are present in anyone's network. Understanding the six stages—and knowing what to do and say at each stage—puts you in charge of the growth and development of your network. As you clarify your goals, you'll network more strategically to achieve them. And sizing your networking Projects to fit your goals will guarantee you get the most from your investment of time and money.

Part III helps you Sharpen Your Skills. Central to our System are the essential face-to-face networking skills that will take you comfortably and professionally from Hello to Goodbye. Because we have worked with people in almost all walks of life, in all kinds of businesses, at every level of the hierarchy, you can be sure that we've covered all the bases. Using focus groups, interviews, and research, we've developed the most complete encyclopedia of real-world, field-tested networking know-how. We've invented models and formulas, collected best practices and examples, created check-lists and quizzes, and identified Frequently Asked Questions and the most common networking dilemmas. As you apply this compre-hensive and practical spectrum of skills, you will be equipped to reach your goals.

Part IV guides you as you Select Your Settings. If you want to network at work, you'll get the tools you need to assess your cor-porate culture, identify key people and activities, and build cross-functional relationships that get things done, affect the bottom line, and advance your career. If you want to network in the world, you'll find the tools to help you choose and get the most out of a variety of venues. You'll maximize the effect of your participation in pro-fessional associations, referral groups, civic and community organi-zations, volunteer and networking activities, at conventions and trade shows, and in social situations.

When you're hunting for a job or want to change careers, we'll coach you to apply your networking skills in well-chosen arenas until you hear the words, "You're hired!"

Survey your skills and mindset, set your strategy, sharpen your skills, and select your settings. Use this system to Make Your Con-tacts Count.

Our best to you,

Anne Baber and Lynne Waymon

P.S.: Contact us at www.ContactsCount.com to tell us about your networking successes.

PART I

Survey Your Skills and Mindset

Start where you are. Check out your mastery of real-world skills. Then, explore your beliefs about networking.

Want to find out how you stack up as a networker? Wonder if you understand the subtleties, know the strategies, and are using state-of-the-art skills? To spotlight your strengths and weaknesses, complete the Self-Assessment in Chapter 1. As you look at your results, you'll be ready to set your priorities and decide which chapters to read first. Then, you'll be able to use your time—and this book—in the best way.

Because you see the marketplace value of networking, you'll want to get rid of any ideas that could hold you back. Misconceptions about networking abound. You can clear your mind of them and adopt attitudes that will get you ready to make great connections.

CHAPTER 1

Assess Your Skills

Taking the Self-Assessment in this chapter will give you an overview of your specific networking behaviors, attitudes, and strategies. This exercise will help you.

▶ Test your current level of mastery of state-of-the-art networking behaviors and beliefs.

▶ Increase your awareness of the vast repertoire of skills and strategies available to you as you build business relationships.

▶ Remind yourself of some techniques that you know but don't use as much as you could.

▶ Pinpoint topics you want to focus on to increase your impact, professionalism, and comfort.

▶ Verify your increased competency when you take the quiz again, after you've made The Contacts Count Networking System a way of life.

Instructions

As you go through the Self-Assessment, we want you to know how we define some of the terms we've used. Then, you'll need to know how to select your answers. Finally, after you are finished with the Self-Assessment, you'll need to know how to assess your mastery and decide what to do next.

Defining Some Terms

Networking Event: All those business, quasi-business, and social situations in which you have opportunities to develop valuable connections.

Organization: Any group you join for the purpose of making business connections (professional association, Chamber of Commerce, alumni group, business referral group, board, etc.).

Company: Who you work for (your firm, your agency, your sole proprietorship, etc.).

Selecting Your Answers

Below, you'll find eight sections: Observing the "Netiquette," Assessing Your Comfort Level, Being Strategic, Meeting People, Using Networking Organizations, Making the Most of Events, Achieving Bottom-Line Results, and Following Through. Each section concentrates on a specific area of the networking experience. The statements in each section focus on what you believe about networking and what you do and say when you are networking. For each statement, check one of the following as your response:

Rarely	for 0 to 20 percent of the time
Sometimes	for 20 to 50 percent of the time
Frequently	for 50 to 80 percent of the time
Almost Always	for 80 to 100 percent of the time

With each section, you'll find a commentary that will help you in your self-assessment.

Observing the "Netiquette"

Look back at your answers as you consider these comments.

If you've ever had an awkward moment as you engaged in a networking activity, you know how daunting it is to feel as if you don't know what to do. As you learn the skills and techniques—and the rationales behind them—you'll find that you'll rarely find yourself in a situation you can't handle with aplomb and confidence.

Handing out lots of business cards isn't networking. See Chapter 6 for the rest of the story.

Observing the "Netiquette"

I talk to discover reasons to hand out my business card.
Rarely _____ Sometimes _____ Frequently _____ Almost Always _____

As I talk with someone, I'm trying to figure out a reason to give him my business card and get his.
Rarely _____ Sometimes _____ Frequently _____ Almost Always _____

I sense when I can begin talking about what I can offer or what my company provides.
Rarely _____ Sometimes _____ Frequently _____ Almost Always _____

I'm comfortable joining a group of people who are already talking.
Rarely _____ Sometimes _____ Frequently _____ Almost Always _____

I consciously work at talking only about 50 percent of the time.
Rarely _____ Sometimes _____ Frequently _____ Almost Always _____

I find interesting ways to say thank you when someone gives me a resource or referral.
Rarely _____ Sometimes _____ Frequently _____ Almost Always _____

If a contact doesn't reciprocate, I skillfully and tactfully point out how she can help me.
Rarely _____ Sometimes _____ Frequently _____ Almost Always _____

Do you worry about seeming too pushy? Too passive? If you're too pushy, you'll turn people off. If you're too passive, you won't get much out of networking.

When you're approaching a group, are you mentally back at the eighth grade dance, wondering if people will snub you? If you know the steps for joining (not breaking into) a group, you'll be able to do it with ease. The process appears in Chapter 6.

Do you, out of nervousness, find yourself chattering away, dominating the conversation? Or do you have a hard time holding up your end of the conversation with Success Stories and important topics to talk about? Give and take is basic to networking. Besides, you have to listen to learn what your contact needs. Chapter 7 will help you avoid all the top 20 networking turn-offs.

Do you say, "Thanks!" in ways that make you memorable, yet are appropriate? Corporate cultures, for example, differ. Appropriate ways to say thank you in IBM are bound to be different from what's done at an ad agency.

Great connectors observe and learn the "netiquette" in particular organizations from the members of those organizations. You can always ask the advice of a mentor at work, when deciding how to say, "Thanks!" Or, you can watch the pros in your association to figure out how quickly it's appropriate to "talk business" with potential clients at the meetings.

Do you sometimes feel that you are the only one in the relationship who is giving? Do you know what to do about that?

Assessing Your Comfort Level

Look back at your answers as you consider these comments.

Networking has emerged as a respected business and career skill. Why, then, does it sometimes feel uncomfortable?

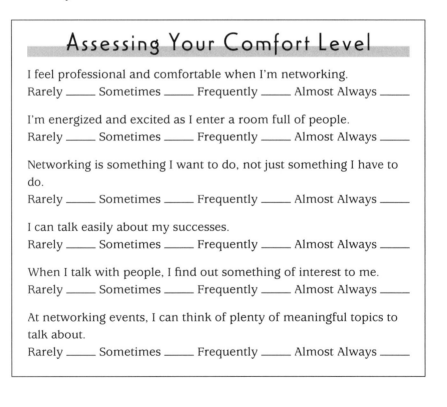

Assessing Your Comfort Level

I feel professional and comfortable when I'm networking.
Rarely _____ Sometimes _____ Frequently _____ Almost Always _____

I'm energized and excited as I enter a room full of people.
Rarely _____ Sometimes _____ Frequently _____ Almost Always _____

Networking is something I want to do, not just something I have to do.
Rarely _____ Sometimes _____ Frequently _____ Almost Always _____

I can talk easily about my successes.
Rarely _____ Sometimes _____ Frequently _____ Almost Always _____

When I talk with people, I find out something of interest to me.
Rarely _____ Sometimes _____ Frequently _____ Almost Always _____

At networking events, I can think of plenty of meaningful topics to talk about.
Rarely _____ Sometimes _____ Frequently _____ Almost Always _____

Few families today sit down to a long Sunday dinner where Uncle Charlie tells stories and Grandma chimes in with reminiscences. Good conversational skills are learned. Few people are born with the gift of gab. But anybody can learn how to use conversation to build networking relationships.

Often, the "ground rules" for networking are unclear. Because it's a "hidden" career and business skill that you're just expected to know, many people are unsure about what's considered professional.

In some circles, networking is mistakenly equated with hot-dogging, tooting your own horn, or grandstanding. Some people say, "I shouldn't have to network. My good work should stand on its own without my having to promote myself." But who will know what you do well and what you need if you don't develop ease in talking about those things? For tips on constructing and telling Success Stories, see Chapter 11.

What happens in the conversation is that after you exchange names and after you ask "What do you do?" there is a pause. It's the pause that comes right before the conversation about the weather. Here's the rule: Never—and we mean never—talk about the weather or the ball scores. Instead, see Chapter 10 to learn how to carry around with you a pocketful of topics you really want to talk about, topics that will convince others of your expertise, build your credibility, teach others to trust you, lead you to resources, and assure that opportunities drop into your lap.

Being Strategic

Look back at your answers as you consider these comments.

Are you surprised that "being strategic" didn't turn out to be one of your strong points? In this sped-up world, it's all too easy to run from activity to event—whatever's available this week will do—and then wonder why networking doesn't work!

So slow down! Make a long-range plan about which Arenas or settings you want to become known in and for what reason. Which organizations should you join? Test drive them before you plunk down the membership dues. There's a quiz that will help you make smart choices in Chapter 17. Want to do Olympic-level networking? Design a Project for yourself that will make you the natural and only choice when opportunity comes knocking.

Being Strategic

I have a long-range, strategic plan for my networking efforts in each organization I belong to.
Rarely _____ Sometimes _____ Frequently _____ Almost Always _____

I join organizations because of my strategic business/career development plan.
Rarely _____ Sometimes _____ Frequently _____ Almost Always _____

Before I go to an event, I think of specific resources/tips/trends I have to offer to the people I'm likely to see there.
Rarely _____ Sometimes _____ Frequently _____ Almost Always _____

I initiate at least one networking meeting (breakfast/lunch, etc.) a week.
Rarely _____ Sometimes _____ Frequently _____ Almost Always _____

I let people know the types of problems I can solve, so they refer exactly the right kinds of opportunities to me.
Rarely _____ Sometimes _____ Frequently _____ Almost Always _____

I'm comfortable telling my contacts what I want or need.
Rarely _____ Sometimes _____ Frequently _____ Almost Always _____

Do you find yourself resisting being strategic? Do you think it's just too calculating to decide on a networking goal and go after it? Do you wish things would "just happen" without your orchestrating them? Tell yourself that managing your networking contacts is okay; manipulating is not. When you are aware of the difference, you'll feel more comfortable making a strategic networking plan. Tell yourself

In networking, strategy equals results.

that planning for visibility and credibility is just like any other planning you do for your business or your career: It makes sense. You have limited hours and dollars to spend in the marketplace, and—without a plan—you'll sink down into aimless activity that doesn't amount to anything.

Meeting People

Look back at your answers as you consider these comments.

Are you surprised that giving your job title isn't the right thing to do? It will be more valuable to you if people know your talent, not your title. As people meet you for the first time, they don't care (yet!) that you're with Smith, Jones, Miller, Barnes and Blarney or that you work for Verizon. To craft answers to the inevitable "What

---

Meeting People

When someone asks, "What do you do?" I avoid giving my job title (e.g., executive vice president of administrative services).
Rarely _____ Sometimes _____ Frequently _____ Almost Always _____

I use several methods to learn people's names.
Rarely _____ Sometimes _____ Frequently _____ Almost Always _____

I've figured out a way to teach others my name and make it memorable.
Rarely _____ Sometimes _____ Frequently _____ Almost Always _____

When I've forgotten someone's name, I know how to retrieve it comfortably.
Rarely _____ Sometimes _____ Frequently _____ Almost Always _____

When someone asks, "What do you do?" I avoid saying, "I'm with . . ." and giving the name of the organization I work for.
Rarely _____ Sometimes _____ Frequently _____ Almost Always _____

When people ask what I do for a living, my answer paints a vivid picture.
Rarely _____ Sometimes _____ Frequently _____ Almost Always _____

When someone asks, "What do you do?" I avoid leading with my occupation or job category (e.g., purchasing agent, lawyer, systems analyst, architect.)
Rarely _____ Sometimes _____ Frequently _____ Almost Always _____

---

do you do?" question that features your talents rather than your title, the name of your company, or your occupation, consult Chapter 9. Hint: Your answers should make it easy for people to talk with you, and should begin to teach people about your Character and Competence.

Have you given up on remembering names? Don't despair. In Chapter 8 you'll find three ways to remember somebody's name and three ways to make your own memorable. That's important too. You'll be pleased to know that there are several things you can do when you forget someone's name besides to say, "Oh, no. I've forgotten your name."

To be a successful networker, you'll have to shed the old meeting/greeting rituals we know so well and do so mindlessly. These rituals restrict, rather than enhance, your ability to build relationships.

Using Networking Organizations

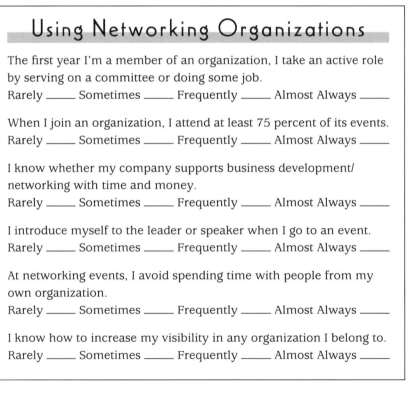

Using Networking Organizations

The first year I'm a member of an organization, I take an active role by serving on a committee or doing some job.
Rarely _____ Sometimes _____ Frequently _____ Almost Always _____

When I join an organization, I attend at least 75 percent of its events.
Rarely _____ Sometimes _____ Frequently _____ Almost Always _____

I know whether my company supports business development/networking with time and money.
Rarely _____ Sometimes _____ Frequently _____ Almost Always _____

I introduce myself to the leader or speaker when I go to an event.
Rarely _____ Sometimes _____ Frequently _____ Almost Always _____

At networking events, I avoid spending time with people from my own organization.
Rarely _____ Sometimes _____ Frequently _____ Almost Always _____

I know how to increase my visibility in any organization I belong to.
Rarely _____ Sometimes _____ Frequently _____ Almost Always _____

Look back at your answers as you consider these comments.

Are you making the most of your memberships? What are the

worst mistakes members make? See Chapter 17. Too often, when it comes to joining organizations, people say, "I'm too busy!" Or "I'm too bashful!" Or "I'm too broke!" If you're in the midst of a job search or starting a business or professional practice, you may wonder if joining is worth the time and money. Well, not if you just join and hang around on the fringes. Not if you spend all your time sitting with and talking to co-workers you see every day. Not if you fail to find ways to exhibit your Character and Competence. Not if you miss opportunities to teach people to trust you.

Do you know how to connect at conventions? If you really want to get your money's worth, see Chapter 19.

Visibility is valuable. You'll find some great ideas about increasing your visibility at work in Chapter 14, and at networking venues in Chapter 17.

Making the Most of Events

Look back at your answers as you consider these comments.

Have you ever left a networking event grumping, "I don't know why I come to these things. I don't get a thing out of them." If you learn the skills in this book, you'll never have that experience again.

Do you want to meet the movers and shakers? Arrive early.

Do you sometimes feel "stuck" talking to the same person long after you've exhausted topics of mutual interest? Most people do. Did you ever say, in leave-taking, "I think I'll go freshen my drink," and head in

How do your skills stack up?

the opposite direction from the bar? You need our easy LEAVE NOW process, described in Chapter 12, so that you know how to end conversations professionally and comfortably. Then you'll be able to move on and meet a dozen people in a two-hour event.

Confused about getting down to business at networking events? Learn how and when to start talking about your company or your product or service.

People want to do business with people they trust. Do your contacts trust you? Do you trust them? What's the key to developing trust? See Chapter 3 for some surprising thoughts on the topic.

Wonder why you should bother to introduce one of your con-

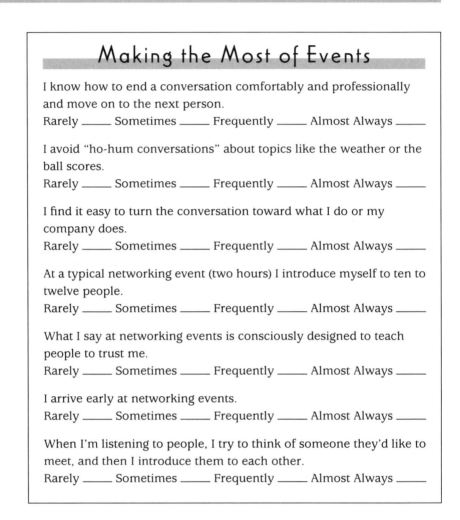

Making the Most of Events

I know how to end a conversation comfortably and professionally and move on to the next person.
Rarely _____ Sometimes _____ Frequently _____ Almost Always _____

I avoid "ho-hum conversations" about topics like the weather or the ball scores.
Rarely _____ Sometimes _____ Frequently _____ Almost Always _____

I find it easy to turn the conversation toward what I do or my company does.
Rarely _____ Sometimes _____ Frequently _____ Almost Always _____

At a typical networking event (two hours) I introduce myself to ten to twelve people.
Rarely _____ Sometimes _____ Frequently _____ Almost Always _____

What I say at networking events is consciously designed to teach people to trust me.
Rarely _____ Sometimes _____ Frequently _____ Almost Always _____

I arrive early at networking events.
Rarely _____ Sometimes _____ Frequently _____ Almost Always _____

When I'm listening to people, I try to think of someone they'd like to meet, and then I introduce them to each other.
Rarely _____ Sometimes _____ Frequently _____ Almost Always _____

tacts to another? Find out the benefits of becoming a great connector, someone known for bringing people together.

Achieving Bottom-Line Results

Look back at your answers as you consider these comments.

This is where the rubber meets the road. The questions in this section reveal whether your network is working.

How about networking at work? Have you detected a resistance to networking inside your corporation, government agency, or insti-

Achieving Bottom-Line Results

After an event, I can name at least three valuable pieces of information I've learned from others.
Rarely ____ Sometimes ____ Frequently ____ Almost Always ____

At work, I hear stories about how people have developed business and enhanced their careers through networking.
Rarely ____ Sometimes ____ Frequently ____ Almost Always ____

I can cite examples of how my networking activities have paid off for my organization.
Rarely ____ Sometimes ____ Frequently ____ Almost Always ____

I can say exactly how my networking activities have paid off for my own career.
Rarely ____ Sometimes ____ Frequently ____ Almost Always ____

I can point out examples of assistance or resources I've given to my contacts.
Rarely ____ Sometimes ____ Frequently ____ Almost Always ____

When I need something, I know whom to call.
Rarely ____ Sometimes ____ Frequently ____ Almost Always ____

When my key contacts talk about me, I notice they can vividly and accurately describe what I do.
Rarely ____ Sometimes ____ Frequently ____ Almost Always ____

tution? Why? How can you decide if your organization (whether you're a sole proprietor or part of a huge corporation) values and supports relationship-building? If you don't know how to read the culture, look at the quiz in Chapter 14. What if networking became "the right thing to do" in your corporate culture? You could help make that happen.

How about you personally? Is your network ready to tap into? Can you point to bottom-line results from specific contacts you've cultivated? When you need a resource, a referral, or an idea—or maybe just a pat on the back—do you know exactly who to call?

How vibrant are your networking relationships? Have you been able to develop a cadre of people who are out in the world promoting you and actively looking for ways to contribute to your success?

Have you ever listened to a contact describe you, your capabilities, your successes to someone else. What a revelation! Use every encounter to teach your contacts something else about you.

Following Through

Following Through

When I get a business card, I put the information in my database.
Rarely _____ Sometimes _____ Frequently _____ Almost Always _____

I Follow Through to provide something I've promised within 3 to 5 days.
Rarely _____ Sometimes _____ Frequently _____ Almost Always _____

Soon after a networking event, I re-connect with two or three people I talked with.
Rarely _____ Sometimes _____ Frequently _____ Almost Always _____

After an event, I have several requests to fulfill from people I talked with.
Rarely _____ Sometimes _____ Frequently _____ Almost Always _____

I am able to fit staying in touch with key contacts into my daily/weekly/monthly routine.
Rarely _____ Sometimes _____ Frequently _____ Almost Always _____

Look back at your answers as you consider these comments.

Wouldn't it be great to Follow Through creatively and consistently? Sure, we recommend that you use an electronic database. But technology isn't the complete answer for keeping in touch. The real key to Following Through is to have something to follow up about. So, be sure that, in addition to talking about yourself, you also find out what's on the other person's Agenda. What are her challenges, interests, needs, enthusiasms, dilemmas? Then you can Follow Through based on her needs, not your need for a new client or your interest in getting a better job. The best relationships are built on giving. When you Listen Generously and focus on giving more than you get, reconnecting becomes a whole lot easier.

Check Your Results

Throughout the Self-Assessment, the best answers are Frequently and Almost Always. Look at your array of answers. If most of your answers are Frequently and Almost Always, you probably have mastered the networking concepts behind the statements. As you go through this book, you will get a kick out of delving deeper into what makes networking work, and you'll pick up some new tips and techniques along the way. If most of your answers are Sometimes and Rarely, you will be saying "Aha!" a lot as you read this book. You'll discover new ideas, new concepts, and, of course, skill-building tips and techniques. Soon you'll be able to put the new ideas to work for you as you build your network.

Next Steps

After you've checked your results in the eight skill areas, take a look at the big picture. Maybe you're doing well in Meeting People, but need to focus on Being Strategic. Or maybe you find that your Comfort Level is high, but you fall down on Following Through. Use this Self-Assessment to set your priorities. Should you go straight to a specific topic or chapter? By giving attention to specific areas, you'll see results quickly. For instance, if the Self-Assessment points out that you need more skill in Meeting People, then you'll want to pay special attention to Chapters 8, 9, and 10. If you find that you were stymied by a majority of the statements, you may decide to start at the beginning of this book and read straight through to the end.

Take out your calendar. Make a note to retake the Self-Assessment in six months. That way, you'll have time to read this book and to put many of the tips and techniques to work. Go ahead. Experiment. Making a small change or adding a new behavior can have a dramatic effect on your ability to connect with people. We predict you'll be pleasantly surprised at how easily you've made the Contacts Count approach to networking a way of life.

CHAPTER 2

Change Your Mindset

What is networking anyhow? It's a term that's been around since the 1960s, but many people still don't have a clear idea of its meaning.

Networking is the deliberate process of exchanging information, resources, support, and access in such a way as to create mutually beneficial relationships for personal and professional success.

That's our official definition, but there's no denying that the term networking has, through the years, collected some negative connotations. What about your mindset? Does networking's chilly image make you freeze up? Could it be that you have some misconceptions about making connections? Do you cringe at the language of networking? Do you think of yourself as shy? Do the things you say to yourself about networking undermine your efforts? In addition to determining what skills you're good at and which ones need sharpening, you also must check out your attitudes. Decide to clear your mind of all the unproductive and debilitating notions that might have crept in. Thinking positively about networking will give you the motivation to leap right in and start learning to be the best that you can be.

Come In from the Cold

What images prevail as people talk about networking? Brrr! People say:

17

▶ "He gave me the cold shoulder."

▶ "What can I say to break the ice?"

▶ "I hate to make cold calls."

▶ "I got cold feet when I thought about going to the meeting alone."

▶ "I just froze up."

It's hard to feel excited about making contact when your mind is full of images like this. If you think of other people—people you might network with—as cold and rejecting, it will be hard for you to enjoy the moment, exchange information, or explore future opportunities.

The Ten Biggest Misconceptions About Networking

1. "I do a good job," says Brad, an engineer. "I shouldn't have to network at work. My work should stand for itself."

Brad's mistaken. Smart employees use networking to stay in touch with internal customers and suppliers. Their networks alert them to problems before they get out of hand and help them spot emerging needs. These employees break through bureaucratic bottlenecks. They use personal contacts to get things moving and speed things up. They build constituencies and gain support for projects and proposals. They collaborate and cooperate. They create ad-hoc, cross-functional, problem-solving teams. When somebody says, "I need it yesterday," they come though. If Brad networked at work, he could serve his organization better and develop his reputation as a person who can get things done—fast.

> **There are no fast-food networks.**

2. "I tried networking last Thursday," says Mel, a franchise owner. "It doesn't work."

To cultivate a bountiful network takes months—maybe even years. Mel has a microwave mentality. You can't zap a relationship for thirty seconds. Networking is a long-term process.

3. "Networking is fine for the junior folks who are still struggling to climb the ladder," says Richard, a vice president of human resources. "But I don't need to network anymore."

No matter what your title, you never outgrow the need to network. Richard could be using networking to his company's—and his—advantage. He could assure his company remains competitive by networking with people who have similar jobs in other companies. Networking is the best way to "benchmark," to check out the best practices and compare yourself with those one rung above you on the corporate ladder. And, the higher up someone is in the hierarchy, the more vulnerable he is. Middle management and staff positions disappear daily. Richard better get cracking to create his "safety net."

> ## You never outgrow the need to network.

4. "Networking is manipulative," says Teresa, who owns a nanny agency. "I don't like the idea of arm twisting someone to do something for me."

True. You can't exploit others and expect to build long-term relationships. The way to avoid manipulation, though, is to give more than you receive. And, when you want something, be up front and overt about it. Look at the following statements. Saying, "To build my business I give free workshops for young parents to show them how to find and manage a nanny. Do you know anyone who'd like an invitation?" will likely prompt a better response than a "hidden agenda" question, such as, "So, do you know anyone with kids under five?"

5. "Networking is just schmoozing," says Karla, a manager of administrative services. "It's boring and . . . uncomfortable."

If Karla's conversations skitter over the surface, she needs to find out how to sidestep those superficialities and get down to business. She can learn how to go beyond the chitchat into conversations that can help her solve problems, come up with new ideas, and access valuable resources.

6. "I'm not looking for a job right now," says Diana, a purchasing manager. "I don't need to network."

Absolutely the worst time to begin networking is when you

need to—after you decide to change jobs or lose your job. If you expect to be job-hunting anytime in the future—and in today's economy, it could be sooner than you think—you should be networking now. The length of your job search depends on the strength of your network. By increasing her visibility among her peers and superiors, Diana can achieve top-of-the-mind awareness. When they think "dynamite purchasing manager," her name will pop up. Not only can networking protect her if her job goes away, it also can lead to new job opportunities—even when she isn't looking.

7. "Networking has never done a thing for me or my career," says Kyle, a director of corporate planning.

That's hard to believe. People can provide access to vital information, such as news of a job opening before it's advertised, insights on industry trends, early warnings of happenings that could impact your business, and even great ideas for a business of your own. Many people can put a bottom-line figure on the value of a single conversation. And sometimes, a single conversation can change your life.

A single conversatio

can change your life

8. "Sure," says Carmen, a photographer. "I know how to network. You just hand out a business card."

Handing out cards isn't networking. Most cards end up in the trash. To network, you must create real, human connections.

9. "I wasn't born with the gift of gab," says Morrie, a CPA. "I'll never be any good at networking."

Only about 10 percent of the people we've interviewed say they come by their conversational skills naturally. The rest of us need networking know-how. Luckily, anyone—even introverts—can learn to network. Once Morrie makes up his mind, he can become better and better at connecting with people.

Networkers are mad,

not born

10. "Networking is a waste of time," says Henri, an attorney. "I leave networking events asking myself, 'Why did I come?'"

More than 85 percent of people who attend networking events tell us they haven't figured out what they want to achieve. If you aim at nothing, you'll hit it, as the saying goes. Henri needs to go with goals in mind. That way, he'll find what he's looking for.

Ten Turnoffs in the Language of Networking

Do the words that people use when they are talking about networking make you cringe? Here's our list of the Top Ten Turnoffs and why we don't like them.

1. "Schmoozing." That word makes networking seem so slimy and insincere!

2. "30-Second Commercial." Sure you want to "sell yourself" to your contact, but this phrase implies too much of a hard sell.

3. "Pick Your Brains." It makes us think of vultures coming in for the kill. We wish people would say, "I'd like to get your thoughts about something."

4. "Work a Room." So depersonalizing and one-sided, this phrase sounds as if you intend to work people over and take all you can.

5. "Information Interview." You don't have to make a specific appointment to gather valuable information. Using state-of-the-art networking skills, you can make networking a way of life.

6. "Tricks of the Trade." Let's not imply anything that smacks of manipulation. There are no "tricks" in our networking System; only upfront, clear offers to be helpful to each other.

7. "Favor Bank." Doing things for others is the right thing; doing things for others just so they'll "owe" you one is the wrong reason to give. Give without strings, without expectations of getting—that's the way to create a network that works.

8. "Power Lunch." Yes, invite a powerful contact to lunch, but don't call it that. It sounds too much as if you value people just for their positions.

9. "Business Card Exchange." Exchanging cards without building trust is non-productive. When you leave a networking event with twenty or thirty cards, what do you do with them? Toss 'em into the trash! Instead, look for reasons to exchange cards. Be alert for ways to move your relationship beyond the networking event into the future. Broadcasting your business cards makes only "cardboard connections," not real connections.

10. "Important People." Don't you hate it when you are talking with someone and that person is looking over your shoulder trying to find someone better to talk with? Give your whole attention to the person you are with. Anyone can turn out to be a wonderful contact!

You Say You're Shy?

Do you think of yourself as shy? You're not alone. The first studies, in 1972 at Stanford University's Shyness Clinic, found that 40 percent of all Americans labeled themselves shy. But, that figure, Clinic Director Dr. Lynne Henderson notes, has steadily increased. Now, as many as 50 percent of us say we're shy.

Philip Zimbardo, who founded the Clinic, blames this rapidly growing fear of being with people on a variety of phenomena—from ATMs to video games to TVs—that reduce day-to-day informal contact with others. And, he says, children don't see their parents relating in a natural, easy, friendly way often enough. Families are smaller and often too busy to spend time honing conversation skills at the dinner table.

Zimbardo defines shyness as reticence and self-consciousness, not just in stressful social situations, but over all. He found that shy people are less popular, find fewer friends, exhibit lower self-esteem, make less money, say their lives are boring, demonstrate fewer leadership skills, are more likely to be depressed, have less social support, and are more likely to be lonely. Shyness will cost you, say these experts. You won't be as successful as someone who has learned to network, make a good appearance, and socialize on the job. Whether you always feel shy or just feel shy in certain situations, you can learn to be more comfortable. "Shyness is not a disease," Henderson says. "It's a habit pattern that can be re-learned."

Remember that many confident, easy-going networkers (including us!) once were shy and uncomfortable. They've just learned new behaviors.

Instead of letting shyness hold you back from networking, learn the skills in this book. You'll become more confident and comfortable and each success will show you the value of connecting.

Catch Your Critic

You climb into your car to go to a networking event. You put your key in the ignition. You turn into the street . . . then, all of a sudden, you're there. You have no recollection of the route you took, the traffic you coped with, or the signs and houses and businesses you passed.

You've been on autopilot. But, when you think about it, you remember that your Critic—the voice in your head—has been ha-ranguing you.

The voice makes it very hard—sometimes impossible—for you to connect easily with others. Notice how your Critic sabotages you.

During introductions, the voice in your head yells at you. Just when the person you're talking with gives his name, the Critic says, "You never can remember people's names." Sure enough, while the Critic is yelling, the other person's name is blotted out.

Bad reviews and bad previews are the Critic's stock in trade.

In the middle of a conversation, the voice mutters, "You never can think of anything to talk about." And guess what . . . it's a self-fulfilling prophecy. You aren't able to think of anything to say.

After you've been talking with someone for several minutes, the voice harangues, "This person would rather be talking to someone more important." And, you fade out of the conversation, stammering something about needing to freshen your drink.

The Critic is bad news. Your brain believes what you tell it about yourself. The good news is you can transform your Critic into a helpful Coach.

If you notice what your Critic says and don't like it, you can reprogram that voice in your head to give you positive and supportive messages instead of negative and defeating ones.

Convert Your Critic into Your Coach

Teach the voice in your head to say something helpful and supportive. Whenever your Critic makes you feel uncomfortable and incapable, develop encouraging statements that make you feel confident and strong. Most of your statements will probably focus on your new beliefs that networking is valuable and that you can learn to do it well.

Changing the way you talk to yourself about your ability to network and combining that new mindset with the specific skills in this book will help you become a better networker. Look at Figure 2-1 for some ideas on how to change that negative Critic into a supportive Coach.

Believe the Best About Yourself and Others

Your beliefs about yourself and other people will support you to succeed at connecting. Take Paul, for example. He used to be appre-

FIGURE 2-1. Turning Your Critic into Your Coach.

Critic	Coach
"I won't be able to think of anything to say."	"I'm good at finding interesting and valuable things to talk about."
"I never remember people's names."	"I bet I can learn five people's names at this event."
"I won't get anything out of this."	"I'm sure the people I meet will turn out to be good contacts."
"Everyone else is better at this than I am."	"I'm getting better and better at this."
"I'll get stuck and won't know how to end the conversation."	"I'm comfortable moving from one conversation to the next."

hensive about entertaining out-of-town clients at dinner. But, to cope with his reluctance about meeting new people, he's gotten in the habit of giving himself a pep talk. "I say to myself, 'They've got kids and hobbies and hopes and dreams.' I think about all the things we have in common. If I prepare, I'm okay."

Paul discovered through experience what psychologists have verified by studying the conversational patterns of people meeting for the first time. These researchers found that if people meeting for the first time believe they have a lot in common, they act very much as if they are old friends. They pay attention to subtle conversational clues and match each other's progress through the conversation. If one brings up a lighter, more informal topic, the other responds with a light topic of his own. If one says something self-revealing, the other follows.

On the other hand, if the strangers are told they have nothing in common, conversation limps along, and both parties feel they haven't connected. This research reinforces the idea that your attitude toward others impacts your success as a networker.

Make up your mind. That will make it a lot easier for you to learn the skills required in today's marketplace.

Bonus: Know Your Style

You don't have to change your personality to be good at networking. Ever taken one of those "communication styles" profiles? Each style has both its comfort zone and its challenge zone. The multitude of communication style assessments on the market today use various terms to help you understand your approach. Whatever assessment you have taken, you should be able to find your profile below.

If you like to head "straight for the finish line," it will feel natural for you to set goals, ask for what you want or need, walk into a room full of strangers, and figure out innovative ways to find good contacts. It will be a challenge for you to slow down and appreciate a conversation partner who has a different style, to take the time to develop trust, to share "air time," and Listen Generously.

If you like to "keep a lot of balls in the air," it will feel natural to you to collaborate, to give first and give generously, and to learn networking skills and systems so that you feel more comfortable. It will be a challenge for you to stick to your goals, to ask for what you want or need, to tell Success Stories, to hold up your end of the conversation, and to take your 50 percent of the "air time."

If you like "hanging out," it will feel natural to you to mix with others, to be enthusiastic when you are talking, and to strike up conversations. It will be a challenge for you to clarify your goals. You'll need to guard against overpowering people, spending too much time talking without focusing on the result you want, and forgetting about your goals because you are enjoying the process of connecting.

If you prefer to "go it alone," it will feel natural to you to plan carefully what you will do at a networking event, to make your Agenda (What to Give and Get), to get one-on-one with people, and to be creative in your approach. It will be a challenge for you to make yourself get out there, to learn to trust others, to demonstrate that you are trustworthy, and to share personal information and Success Stories.

If you like "taking things easy," it will feel natural to you to Listen Generously to your partner, to feel that networking is cooperating not competing, to save time by targeting your networking and to set goals. It will be a challenge for you to respond quickly in conversations, to focus on your needs and wants, and to feel a sense of urgency to get things done.

If you like to "floor it," it will feel natural to you to seek out a variety of people and organizations, to enjoy the excitement of making those initial contacts, and to have lots of irons in the fire. It will be a challenge for you to be strategic, to Follow Through to deepen your contacts, to focus and concentrate on selected contacts rather than continuing to seek new ones, to limit the number of organizations you are a member of, and to take the time to develop trust.

If you like to get "your ducks in a row," it will feel natural to you to use The Contacts Count Networking System—to learn the steps to become a more skillful networker, to practice your skills, to appreciate the Give/Get concept of networking because it's fair, and to keep track of your contacts and networking activities. It will be a challenge for you to get started, to keep from worrying about being perfect, to quit being concerned about meeting the "right people."

If you like to "go with the flow," it will feel natural to you to be upfront about what you want and need, to appreciate the Contacts Count System's non-manipulative approach, to be candid with contacts to move relationships forward, and to give up the tired, old rituals we use when meeting people. It will be a challenge for you to focus on the details of making and maintaining contact, to Follow Through effectively and systematically, and to develop relationships over the long haul.

You don't have to change who you are. Whatever your style, know that you can customize all the ideas in this book to enhance who you already are.

PART II

Set Your Strategy

The biggest mistake networkers make is not being strategic. To be strategic, you must understand and use two underlying concepts: How trust develops and how relationships develop. These unique Contacts Count ideas will provide a strong base for all your networking activities. Then you can create the goals and Projects that get you where you want to go.

Do you know that trust building is *the* most important networking activity? Even if you realize its importance, you may not know how to do it. What do you know about trust? We break it down into its two essential components—Character and Competence—and show you how to demonstrate them in every encounter.

Do you have a binary approach to networking? Do you think people are either a part of—or not a part of—your network? Networking relationships are much more complex than that. You can plot each one of your contacts on the Six-Stages Model. Once you know where they are on this map, you'll immediately be able to see what you can do next to enhance those relationships. You'll understand your relationships and how to develop them in a new way that makes re-connecting and staying in touch easy—and more and more beneficial for both you and your contacts.

Want to get the biggest bang for your networking buck? Create the networking Project that will take you to your goal.

CHAPTER 3

Teach Trust

Everybody says, "People want to do business with people they trust."

Have you ever been at a networking event where someone came up to you and introduced himself saying, "Hi, I'm George. I sell long-term care insurance. Do you need any?"

It's this kind of "going for the jugular" that gives networking a bad name. You don't know or trust George enough to do business with him.

Trust is the outcome of several (our research indicates six to eight) conversations in which you provide examples of your trustworthiness and observe your contact's behavior and listen to what he says to determine if he can be trusted.

People teach people to trust them.

If Peter, a career coach, takes sloppy minutes at the committee meeting, or forgets to return JoAnn's phone call, or has a couple of typos in his marketing brochure, JoAnn probably won't hire him. Nor will she recommend him to her friends and acquaintances.

On the other hand, if he handles his committee responsibilities carefully, and promptly returns calls, and has professional looking marketing materials, then JoAnn will probably think of him when she decides to make a career change and needs some help.

After JoAnn becomes Peter's client, if she cancels sessions at the last minute, fails to follow through on her "homework" that will help him guide her job hunt, and looks as if she came straight from her workout at the health club, Peter will be reluctant to recommend her for a job he knows about.

If JoAnn arrives on time, dresses professionally, completes all of the assessments Peter has provided, and speaks positively about her expertise and her current employer, then Peter probably will pass along the job lead.

Move from Taking to Trusting

As people begin to network, they typically focus on trying to get something for themselves. There's nothing wrong with wanting your efforts to bear fruit. But, that's only part of the story. Networking is not just about TAKING.

The TAKING mindset works when you happen to connect with somebody who has what you want or needs what you're offering.

George, the guy who sells long-term care insurance, is focusing on TAKING. He's only interested in you if you, at that very moment, in the middle of the Chamber of Commerce's "Business After Hours" event, let's say, happen to need long-term care insurance and are willing (remarkably!) to buy it from him. His approach is no more than a face-to-face cold call. Chances are he'll go home after the event and grump, "This networking stuff is a bunch of hooey!"

Charlene went to that same Chamber event thinking about a problem: how to ship a fragile antique desk to her daughter in London. When she asked Bart, whom she'd just met, what he did, he said, "I ship anything anywhere, especially valuable things. I just sent a baby grand to the Philippines." Bingo!

But if that's the only kind of networking you are ready to do, you are not going to be very satisfied. During that networking event that lasted two hours and involved more than 800 people, how many serendipitous meetings like Charlene and Bart's do you think happened? Probably not very many.

When you begin to realize that the point of networking is to exchange something of value, you've begun to think of networking as TRADING.

TRADING is exciting. It makes you feel as if your networking efforts are worthwhile. Clarice, who has her own training company, went to a networking breakfast and met the college-age son of a member. She was delighted to meet Howie, who has a window-washing business, because she needed that service immediately. She took Howie's card so she could call him and get an estimate. When Howie found out what Clarice did, he suggested she talk with his dad because he knew his father's company was looking for someone to write a training manual. That's a great trade. But it's a one-time trade. Clarice will need her windows washed only once in a blue moon. Howie's business may not last beyond the summer, and he may not know anyone else who might need her training services.

When people think of networking as TAKING or TRADING, what they get is Single-Sale Networking. Though Single-Sale Networking may result in instant gratification, it's time-consuming, and you miss out on the long-term benefits. Unfortunately, many people feel that when they have achieved a TRADE, they have reached the epitome of networking.

> **Networking isn't about taking; it's about teaching.**

Long-term networking relationships are built by TEACHING people what you need and what to count on you for, and by learning the same about them. When you meet someone, take the time to be interested in that person and his or her business. Put your antenna up for resources, ideas, tips, information, or access that you could give to that contact. Look for ways to become known to that person and to educate that person about yourself and your capabilities.

Remember the old line: "It's not WHAT you know, it's WHO you know?" That's only partly true. Sure, WHAT you know is important. It's your expertise, your knowledge, what you are paid for. WHO you know is important, too. Those are the people you call when you are looking for an idea, a resource, a referral.

But just as important as WHAT you know and WHO you know is WHO KNOWS YOU. Does Fred know you so well that, when something comes into his life, you pop into his head. And he says to himself, "Oh, I've got to send this to Sean." Who knows you that well?

The big networking challenge, then, is how to teach your contacts who you are and what you are looking for, so they can send good things your way. An equally big challenge is how to learn about your contacts and what they are looking for, so you can send good things their way. Make sure you spend as much time learning about your contact's business and life as you do teaching him or her who you are.

When you put your emphasis on developing TRUST, then relationships become mutually beneficial.

Teach That You Can Be Trusted

Your contacts will begin to trust you as you teach them about your Character and Competence. To teach your contacts about your Character:

▶ Do what you say you will do.

▶ Meet deadlines.

▶ Go for the win/win solution.

▶ Treat everyone you meet fairly.

▶ Be unfailingly reliable.

▶ Speak well of people even when they are not present.

▶ Come from a position of abundance, not scarcity.

▶ Collaborate rather than compete.

▶ When something goes wrong, ostentatiously make it right or compensate generously for your failure.

▶ Go the extra mile.

▶ Respect other people's time and possessions.

To believe in your Character, your contacts must either see you in action (observe your behavior) or must hear about you (listen to stories you tell about yourself that provide vivid examples of your Character).

If you promise your contact you'll call her on Tuesday, do it. That's how you teach someone that you will do what you say you will do.

If you promise you'll come up with ten items for the public television fund-raising auction by December 5, provide a dozen. That's how you teach someone that you meet deadlines, are reliable and go the extra mile.

Suppose you want to teach someone that when something goes

wrong, you'll do more than make it right. Tell about the time you inadvertently charged a customer more than you should have for a job and how, when you discovered the mistake, you not only called to apologize and to ask if he would like his money returned or credited to his account, but also sent him a basket of cookies as an additional apology.

Suppose you want to teach someone that you're a stickler for details. Talk about the newsletter you edit for your professional association. Tell how you go to great lengths to be sure every name is spelled correctly and all details in the articles are correct.

> **Your contacts won't help you until they trust you.**

Suppose you want to teach someone that you are innovative. Tell about your work on the program committee that's resulted in an award-winning line-up of programs for the association.

Suppose you want to teach someone that you are a good organizer. Tell about the time you compiled information to submit to national to enter the Chapter of the Year contest. (See Chapter 11 for more ideas on using stories to teach about yourself.)

To teach your contacts about your Competence, you will need to reveal that you:

▶ Have earned the proper credentials.

▶ Stay at the leading edge of your profession.

▶ Have won praise and awards from your peers.

▶ Take life-long learning seriously.

▶ Are cited as an expert in the trade press or in the mass media.

▶ Teach or mentor others.

▶ Consult with others to share your expertise.

▶ Write for publication or speak in public.

▶ Do the job right—the first time.

▶ Are happy to discuss your procedures and processes with clients and customers.

▶Handle "the little stuff" with care.

▶Follow through to be sure that your work meets or exceeds expectations.

Here are some suggestions about ways to show your Competence: Frame diplomas, accreditation certificates, and customer kudos and hang them on the wall of your office. Invite your contact to lunch and give her the "grand tour." Send contacts articles that quote you, newspaper clippings or conference programs that show you speaking. Tell stories (See Chapter 11.) about consulting with others. Protect the confidentiality of the organization or person you consulted with. Tell other stories about doing the job right and handling "the little stuff" with care. Provide your contact with a sample of your work or a tour of your work site.

To build a strong network, make sure your contacts know your capabilities and are confident in your ability to perform. It's unreasonable to expect that people who don't know you will be comfortable giving you referrals or suggesting you for jobs. They have no idea of your special areas of expertise and have not known you long enough to be sure you will come through.

Use a similar process to learn about your contact's Character and Competence: look for the same behaviors and ask for stories.

The Trust Matrix

The Trust Matrix, shown in Figure 3-1, graphically depicts the process of developing trust. When you first meet someone, you probably have little knowledge of his Competence and Character. And your contact probably doesn't know how you would rate in those areas either. That's why most relationships begin in the lower left quadrant of The Trust Matrix, with Competence and Character still to be determined. You are Acquaintances.

If a contact has a "bad experience" with you—or if you have a "bad experience" with your contact—your relationship will derail into the upper left quadrant or the lower right quadrant.

If your relationship moves to the upper left quadrant, your contact trusts your Character, but questions your Competence. He thinks you are Admirable But Not Able. This situation can be remedied. It could be that you have just changed jobs or just graduated

FIGURE 3-1. The Trust Matrix.

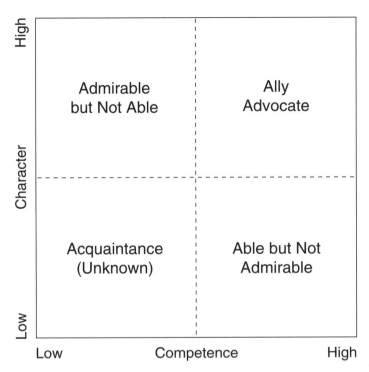

and are in your first job or have moved into a new career field. Think about how you can teach your contact that you are Able—or Competent—as well as Admirable. Tell stories as you talk or send out a newsletter or press release to let contacts know about your increasing expertise. Take a visible role in organizations, so contacts can experience your Competence first hand.

If your relationship moves to the lower right quadrant, your contact trusts your Competence, but questions your Character. Your contact believes you are Able But Not Admirable. Everybody makes mistakes that contribute to concerns about Character or Competence. Can you repair the mistake and your reputation? If you were late to an event, show over time that lateness was a one-time aberration, not a habit. You will have to demonstrate repeatedly that your character is Admirable.

If you have positive experiences with each other, your networking relationship will move to the top right quadrant. You will become Advocates or Allies. Advocates speak well of you and your business, refer qualified customers or clients to you and create opportunities for you. Allies are trusted advisors. Your trust in the confidentiality of the relationship and the value of the relationship is so high that you feel comfortable sharing frustrations and trade secrets, and celebrating successes. Developing that level of trust takes time.

It's also possible that one or both of you may have established a reputation in the community. Ideally, you want contacts to hear good things *about* you before they hear *from* you. If your good reputation precedes you, your relationship may start off in the upper right hand quadrant. If so, you've "jump started" the process and can begin your relationship with Character and Competence assumed. That doesn't mean that you can relax and forget about the trust question. As your relationship continues, continue to reaffirm both your Character and Competence.

Avoid Manipulation

Networking is not about manipulating other people. If you are absolutely honest about what you want to establish—a mutually beneficial, long-term, trusting, business relationship—you will not be manipulating your contacts. It's only when you connive to get something for yourself through misdirection, subterfuge, or telling only part of the truth that you are being manipulative. Don't do it. (See Chapter 10 for a more detailed discussion of the dangers of manipulation.) To build trust, you must convince your contact of your Character, as well as your Competence. Nothing destroys relationships quicker than one party feeling manipulated by the other. Be totally upfront about your motives.

CHAPTER 4

Develop Your Relationships

Networks are always becoming. They are never complete or static. Networking relationships offer the possibility of growth through six stages of development. Understanding these stages will help you figure out what behaviors are professional—not too pushy and not too passive. You'll be able to assess your current network and decide where to put your energies to widen and strengthen it.

Make a list of ten people you know. Include a variety of people: co-workers; people you know well and people you have just met; clients, customers, or vendors; people from a professional association or community organization; people from your leisure life. Keep these people in mind as you read about the Six Stages.

Move Through the Six Stages

Study the Six-Stages Model, shown in Figure 4-1. On the outside are all the people you run into, however casually. At the center are those few people with whom you have very trusting and long-term relationships.

Accidents. In your lifetime, you will bump into thousands of people. These casual, unplanned, random encounters are Accidents. They probably will never be repeated. They are one-time-

FIGURE 4-1. The Six Stages Model.

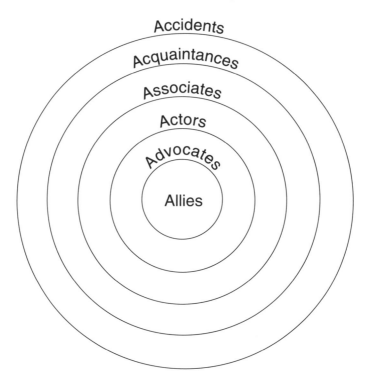

only meetings. You are thrown together for some period of time. So you talk to each other—in line for tickets to the hit play, in the emergency room waiting area, when you are 14C and she is 14B on the plane. Any person you meet outside a common context is an Accident. Networking relationships sometimes grow out of Accidents if you can find a reason to stay in touch.

Acquaintances. People that you run into because of who you are and what you do are Acquaintances. They have something in common with you. An Acquaintance may be a person who is a friend of a friend. You meet at your neighbor's daughter's wedding, for instance. You *might* see an Acquaintance again. Then again, you might not. There's enough of a connection there that, if you *had* to, you could probably find an Acquaintance again.

When someone mentions your Acquaintance Ramon Sanchez to you, you're likely to say, "Ramon Sanchez? Sounds familiar. I think I've met him. Isn't he a lawyer or a CPA or something like that?" He'd probably be as vague about you. You may be able to recall an Acquaintance's name, but you haven't really begun to learn about each other.

Associates. People you come in contact with on some regular basis for some period of time are Associates. You are both part of the same system. You've both joined the alumni association, or the swim club, or a professional association, or you work for the same employer. Because you see each other every week or every month—or even every year—you have the chance to learn each other's names and reconnect often enough to learn a bit about each other. But unless both of you work at the relationship, it will never develop. You will continue to see each other, chat briefly, and part, without providing any assistance to each other.

If Ramon has become an Associate, you might describe him like this: "Ramon is a attorney. He's a member of our Chamber. I think he specializes in estates. I could find him in the membership directory."

Actors. People with whom you exchange valuable information, resources, or leads are Actors. Sometimes you are the giver in the exchange; sometimes you are the receiver. Whether you realize it or not, you are looking for two things in each other. If you each find these two things, you'll want more activity with each other; if you don't see these two things exhibited in their conversation and behavior, you won't pursue the relationship. What are these two things? Character and Competence. (See Chapter 3.)

You gather information about each other and have each other's phone numbers and e-mail addresses. You know enough about him, and he knows enough about you, to be useful to each other. Once you get into an exchange relationship, you are Actors.

If you needed to find someone to advise you on setting up a trust, you might say, "Oh, Ramon. I met him at the Chamber." Once you make an appointment with Ramon, you become Actors. You make note of his phone number and address. When you meet with him, you look for evidence of his Character and Competence and begin to demonstrate yours.

Advocates. People who believe in each other's Character and Competence are Advocates. You know that your Advocates will come through, and they know that you will help them. You have developed a high level of trust with each other. Your antenna is up for information and resources for these people. And they, likewise, feed you opportunities. You speak well of them.

When Ramon becomes an Advocate, you look for ways to assist him. If someone mentions that she is concerned about how well organized her Mother's financial situation is, you recommend Ramon, saying, "I worked with an excellent attorney, Ramon Sanchez, who helped my mother set up a trust. Why don't you give him a call? I know his first consultation is free. I recommend him highly. You can reach him at this number."

Allies. People who are experts on you, your business, your career, your needs, your aspirations, and your vision are Allies. They know where you've been and where you're headed—and they want to help you get there! They are your senior advisors, and you are theirs. Because you talk about core life and business issues, you have established confidentiality as a ground rule of your relationship. You both are so committed to your mutual success that you serve on each other's unofficial Board of Directors. These are the people you turn to for sage advice—on how to climb the corporate ladder, on whether it's time to open a branch office in Denver, on how to deal with a difficult client. Allies commiserate with you when the going gets rough and celebrate with you when success is sweet.

When Ramon becomes an Ally, you might call and say, "Hey, Ramon, your daughter's wedding was beautiful. By the way, I know of a board opening that might be a good career move for you. Do you want me to give your name to the chairman? Also, let's get together next week. I'm thinking of making some big changes, and I'd like your thoughts."

Go back to that list of ten people you made. Decide what stage you are at with each person on your list. Assuming that your list of ten is representative of all the people you know, what does it tell you about how you need to expand and develop your network? What does it tell you about appropriate next steps with these ten people? If you made an even broader list of people you know, would there be a good mix of people from a variety of Arenas? Would it include people from your workplace, your profession, your industry, your friendship and leisure-time circle, your family?

The Next Move Is Up to You

As you look at the Six-Stages Model, you'll become clear about what you need to do if you'd like to have more of a relationship with someone. Look at Figure 4-2 for further ideas on transitioning from one Stage to the next.

If you and Jim are Associates, your Number One job is to Listen Generously, so you can find out what he needs. When you find something that you can give, you will just naturally move to the Actor stage of exchanging.

If you and Monica are Actors, your Number One job is to show her your Character and Competence through everything you do and say.

If you and Horatio are Advocates, your Number One job is to promote him and to keep your antenna up for opportunities and possibilities to pass along to him.

If you and Svetlana are Allies, your Number One job is to tell the truth, provide support for all she does, and help her in any way you can to succeed in both her business and personal life.

You'll probably have hundreds or thousands of Accidents, Acquaintances, and Associates in your lifetime. You'll enter into an Actor relationship with fewer people, and even fewer will become

FIGURE 4-2. Next Steps.

If you want more Associates	Make strategic decisions about which organizations to join based on your career, business and life goals.
If you want to move from Associate to Actor	Listen Generously so you can give ideas, resources, and referrals.
If you want to move from Actor to Advocate	Show your Character and Competence in everything you do and say.
If you want to move from Advocate to Ally	Introduce your Advocate to all parts of your life, be in touch frequently, give generously, offer support.
If you want to be a strong Ally	Respect confidentiality, tell the truth with caring, help with challenges, and celebrate your Ally's success in life and business.

Advocates and Allies. Of course, you can't make anyone move to the next stage with you, but you can say and do things that will make it more likely that the relationship will grow.

Rate Your Relationships

Networking is a process of teaching and learning. Choose someone on your list of ten and use this quiz to figure out where you are with that person. When you answer "No," you'll have a clue about what you want to be sure to tell—and ask—the next time you meet.

1. Does she recognize my name instantly when I call?

2. Does she know me well enough to recognize me "out of context," at the store, in a new group?

3. Does she know my face and my name well enough to come up to me in a crowd and introduce me accurately to others?

4. Has she found a reason to have my phone number or e-mail in her system?

5. Does she know the name of my company or organization?

6. Can she accurately describe what I do?

7. Can she give vivid examples of what I do?

8. Does she know that I am good at what I do and can she cite reasons why my service, product, or skills are superior?

9. Does she know of some independent verification of my expertise such as an award, a certification, or a third party endorsement?

10. Does she regularly send me valuable information and respond to requests from me?

11. Does she know what kind of customers, clients, or job opportunities will appeal to me and does she send them my way?

12. Does she always speak well of me to other people and pass my name around?

13. Does she regularly refer qualified customers, clients, or job opportunities to me?

14. Does she consistently create opportunities to stay in touch with me?

15. Does she treat the business, career, and life issues we talk about with confidentiality and caring?

This quiz highlights our finding that it often takes six or eight contacts with someone before he or she knows who you are, has learned your marketplace niche, and begins to trust you. Once that trust is established, you might be in touch once a week or once a year, depending on the relationship.

In networking, the ball's always in your court. It's up to you to take the next step to cultivate the relationship.

Have Questions About the A's?

Here are some of the questions people have about the Six Stages.

Q: "I have two Advocates and they don't like each other. What can I do?"

A: Say to each of them separately, "I know you two don't see eye-to-eye. That's a huge advantage to me because I get two distinct points of view. I wish you could bury the hatchet, but if not, I'll still value advice and input you both give me."

Q: "I've made some incredible contacts with Accidents. I got a $50,000 training contract because I said hello to a fellow passenger in the van from the airport to the hotel. Why bother to cultivate long-term relationships when that works so well?"

A: Making a magical connection with someone you meet on the fly (no pun intended) is great fun. But, over the long haul, you'll be glad to have the mature and solid, mutually beneficial relationships with Advocates and Allies. You'll get more than business from them; you'll get support and opportunities that are tailor-made for you, because they know you so well.

Q: "Can customers and clients become Advocates and Allies? I guess we became Actors when I worked for them but that was four years ago. We have no relationship now."

A: Sure they can. When you add buying and selling into the relationships, they become more complex. If both parties are of high Character and Competence, and if both are candid and open, the relationship can flourish.

Q: "I heard that people often get jobs from secondary contacts. That sounds like the Acquaintances stage would bring the most benefits."

A: You're right. If you are job hunting, it would be wise to seek out those Acquaintances—friends of friends—because they move in different Arenas than you do. That means when you contact them you expand your network. You have another advantage with Acquaintances: they give you trust because they trust your mutual friend or contact.

Q: "When I looked at my ten people versus the Six-Stages Model, all were Associates. What am I doing wrong?"

A: This situation is typical for younger networkers who haven't had the time—or perhaps the need—to build a network to help them advance their careers. First, you may simply have been thinking of groups you belong to as you made your list of ten. That would have led you to write down mostly Associates. Second, you may need to do more than join organizations. You may need to work at your network to deepen those relationships.

Q: "I thought of ten people, but my best contacts are my friends. Do my friends fit on that model? Or are they outside?"

A: Again, this situation is typical of networkers early in their careers. They're still hanging around with college buddies or people they grew up with. It's great to think of friends as networking contacts. Have conversations with them about keeping your antennas up, so you can provide opportunities for each other. And certainly, when you become Allies with someone, they become friends because you have shared your personal and career goals. It's wise however, to cultivate contacts strategically—to specialize a bit—so that you meet people in your career field or profession.

Q: "I have people that I think of as Actors because I've done something for them, but they never do anything for me. How can I not only move to the next stage with them, but also be sure that the relationship is mutually beneficial?"

A: Think about these people—the networking moochers in your life—as you answer the questions on the Rate Your Relationships quiz. Perhaps you haven't taught them what you're looking for and how they might be helpful. Next time you meet, have a couple of Success Stories to tell them, so that they can better appreciate your abilities and amiability. If you continue to feel that they aren't reciprocating, have a conversation in which you recount some of the things you've done for them and say, "Here's how you could help me." If that doesn't work, cross them off your list. There are a lot of people out there who will be happy to reciprocate.

Q: "There's an Associate of mine that I don't want to have a relationship with at all. He's not a person whose ethics I admire. But he keeps calling and wanting to get together. What should I do?"

A: Be busy when he calls, very busy.

Q: "I think I have all Advocates and Allies in my network."

A: Check it out by having conversations with some of these people and asking them, for example, to give a vivid example of what you do. If they can't, tell them Success Stories. They'll be likely to remember those anecdotes. Ask yourself if you are suffering from Tired Network Syndrome. You may have been at it so long, that you do have a cadre of well-established relationships. On the other hand, do you have networking needs that they are unable to fulfill—new passions in your life that your current contacts are not connecting with? If so, deliberately set out to join some new Arenas and meet some people who can share your new interests.

Q: "How much time does it take to develop and nurture a relationship with an Ally?"

A: Lots. Because you are so in tune, you may be tempted to cut back on the time you spend with these valuable contacts. Be sure that you do set aside a regular time to get together, perhaps dinner once a month. Challenge yourself to find some way that you can contribute to their success every time you meet. Listen Generously, be Seriously Curious and swap Success Stories. Then you'll be able to profit from—and continue to enjoy—those relationships for years to come.

CHAPTER 5

Go with Your Goals

Networking is small talk with a purpose. What's yours? What's going on in your life that makes you ready to work on your network?

You may have a vague notion that "Things go better with networking." You're right. Networking is not just a career skill; it's a life skill. It's for new grads, for people at any stage of their careers—or even for retirees. If you've decided that you want to know how to network better just because it's the smart thing to do, leap right in.

You may already have a personal goal—one that has nothing to do with your career. Perhaps you've decided you want to find a significant volunteer activity, something you can do to make a difference. You may already have a career goal. Perhaps you want to take the certification program offered by your professional association. You may already have a business goal. Perhaps you want to create a partnership with another entrepreneur. You may already have a workplace goal. Your organization may have announced initiatives that make building relationships a priority. Any goal you have can be the impetus for a networking Project.

Size Your Project to Match Your Goal

You are CEO, president, and chairman of the board of your network. You will customize it to fit your own needs. It won't be a carbon copy of anybody else's network. It will include a unique set of contacts developed for your unique set of reasons. You will construct your network and select networking activities to move toward your goal, whatever it is.

If your goal is small, it might require only a small networking Project—one that can be accomplished in less than six months and is made up of only a couple of activities. It will take only a limited number of networking contacts and a limited amount of money, time, and effort. Wanting to benchmark your department's processes and procedures, for example, you might put together a group of several people in your professional association who have similar jobs. As each person hosts one meeting and provides an overview of his department, you'll all get a better idea of how your workplaces measure up.

> **Never underestimate the power of networking to enhance your life, both professionally and personally.**

If your goal is medium-sized, it might require a larger networking Project—one that could take six months to a year, with a corresponding outlay of money, time, and effort. Say you want to fulfill your department's new objective: Raise the visibility of our bank with small business owners. You will create a networking Project that includes a variety of substantial activities. You might join the Chamber and immediately volunteer for a committee that is assessing Chamber programs that target small businesses. And you might put together—and get bank sponsorship for—a workshop for members of the Home-Based Business Association. Over time, you will be able to open up many opportunities to meet small businesses owners.

If your goal is very far-reaching, you'll need to create a large-scale networking effort. It might take several years and require commitment, perhaps even self-sacrifice, not to mention money and time! These big, long-term, life-changing efforts are Strategic Positioning Projects. They will include many kinds of networking activities, pursued with high intensity. They will position you to be the natural and only choice when opportunity knocks.

Check Out Your Choices

Whatever the size of your networking effort, you'll come to many ChoicePoints along the way. These are opportunities to make strategic decisions about what you will say or do. As you make these decisions, your goal is a guidepost showing you the right direction. Think, for example how many ChoicePoints—strategic decisions—you'll deal with as you attend just one networking event. You'll decide:

▶ What you want to get out of the event.

▶ What information you are prepared to give

▶ Who to talk with

▶ How to make your name memorable

▶ What to talk about

▶ What stories to tell that show what kind of expertise

▶ Whose cards to get and keep

▶ When you want to leave a conversation

And that's only a partial list. Using all the tips, tactics, and tools in this book will help you manage the many ChoicePoints and make the right decisions, every time.

Assess Your Network

Before you begin to set the parameters for your networking Project, look at what you are currently doing and already have in place. Then you'll be able to decide what your networking Project will look like, what your investment will be, and how you can build on your existing circles.

Tally your time. Grab a piece of paper and a calculator, and tally up the time you currently devote to networking. Consult your calendar for the previous twelve months. Can you document how much of your own and your employer's time you have spent? In our workshops, we've heard people say everything from a low of 20 hours a year to a high of 600 hours a year (about 12 hours a week). Of course, people in some careers spend almost all of their time networking.

Calculate the cash. Now, figure out how much money you (and your organization) spent on your networking last year. Include dues and other expenses for activities, such as associations, professional groups, referral groups, country clubs, conferences, business lunches, trade shows, sports boxes and tickets, etc. Include money out of your own pocket, as well as money spent by your organization. What's the grand total of your financial commitment? We've heard amounts that ranged from a measly $75 to a grand $75,000.

Determine your return. Are you surprised to see how *little* time and money you actually spend, given how important meeting new people and re-connecting with long-time contacts are to your goals? Or are you shocked to realize how *much* time and money you spend and want a better return on your investment? Do you need to increase the effectiveness of your networking to get your money's worth?

Decide on your investment. How much time and money should you ideally spend? This is an important decision to make as you tune into your goals and begin to think what size networking Projects you want to do. You can't expect to spend five minutes and five bucks and change your life through networking. On the other hand, you can easily overspend or waste your hard-earned dollars or overextend yourself and waste your valuable time, if you don't make strategic decisions about where and when to spend your time and money. The bigger your goal, the more you are going to have to put into your networking efforts to achieve it.

Add up your Arenas. Your Arenas are the circles you are known in and the groups you belong to. To maximize your opportunities for building your network, we recommend that you take part in six different Arenas.

Adele's Arenas

Adele is a lawyer who specializes in serving clients in the high-tech industry. She has two goals: to gain "key player" status in that industry for her firm and, since she's in charge of her firm's new hire program, to increase by 25 percent the number of women associates hired over the next three years. Figure 5-1 is a chart she made of her involvement in six different Arenas.

Your Turn

Create a chart like the one in Figure 5-1 and list all of your Arenas. First, list the Arenas you're already a part of because of who you

FIGURE 5-1. Adele's Arenas.

Organization	Role	Benefit	Reason
University of Maryland Alumni Association	Member. (Rarely attend.)	See people from all walks of life. Service to alma mater.	Meet potential clients. Look for new hires.
Northern Virginia Technology Council	Long-Range Planning Committee Chair. (Attend 2 meetings a month.)	Hot information. A chance to show problem-solving and leadership skills.	Become President to gain industry visibility.
Greater Washington Board of Trade	Vice-President.	Wide visibility with 1,200 member companies.	Develop collaboration with and referrals from CPA firms. Meet potential clients.
Women in Technology	Member. (Attend 3 times a year.)	Updates on current trends.	Look for new hires.
Dingman Center for Entrepreneurship at the University of Maryland	Lecturer.	Visibility, prestige.	Refine public speaking skills.
Maryland Bar Association	Member.	Professional development.	Referrals; update credentials.

are and what you already do. These Arenas have no membership dues, but they are circles of people you know: "I'm a parent who knows the parents of the other kids in my daughter's ballet class" or "I know my neighbors in Post Oak Farms." Then add the organizations you've paid to become involved with.

Fill out the rest of your chart. Make a note about the nature of your participation—what Role you play. Be honest. If you only attended two events last year, put that down. Then, itemize the Benefits of each organization. Do the Benefits of belonging contribute to the networking Project you are putting together to reach your goal? Finally, fill in your Reasons for belonging to that organization. Again, you may find that an organization is not a good fit for the direction that you are trying to go. Use your chart to assess the value to you of the organizations you belong to.

Assess the benefits. Are you getting what you want from these organizations? If not, are they the wrong ones for you or do you need to find more strategic ways to participate? Does being involved contribute to your goals or have you outgrown your need for and interest in the group? Don't start joining new Arenas if you have not taken advantage of the opportunities in groups you're already a part of. As you assess your Arenas, ask yourself, "Where have I developed the most profitable contacts in the past?"

As Adele looked over her involvements, she decided that although Alumni Association events were fun, she'd be more likely to find clients and women to hire in other places. She was satisfied with what she was doing in the Technology Council. She noticed that her reason for joining the Board of Trade—contact with CPA firms—was not at the top of her list of current goals, but remembered several new clients in recent months had come from the group. As she thought about Women in Technology, she decided to consult the membership directory to see just how many lawyers were members. She found only four. None were a good fit with her law firm. She decided to terminate her membership. As she thought about the Dingman Center, she realized that, having lectured there for three years, she had already become an accomplished speaker and needed to find new reasons for continuing to teach there. She felt the Bar Association was a must.

As Adele assessed her involvements, she saw how important it is to make sure that organizations you belong to are the right ones for your networking Project.

Find new Arenas. When you decide it is time to choose a new Arena, ask yourself, "Whom would I like to meet, and where can I find that type of person?" Look at the guidelines in Chapter 17.

Plan Your Strategic Positioning Project

Here's how to get started planning your big Project to reach your big goal. If your goal is smaller, just scale down the networking activities you undertake.

Go for quantity as you come up with networking options to pursue your Strategic Positioning Project. You can put together a group to help you brainstorm. Or glean ideas from stories in the business press, from *The Wall Street Journal* to *Fast Company*. Or ask colleagues or mentors for ideas. Or borrow models or adapt ideas from what others have done. You'll find dozens of ideas throughout this book.

Use your network within your organization, your community, your profession, or your industry to do

> **Design a big-time, long-term Project.**

some preliminary research about possible activities. Then, outline your networking options. Projects evolve. You'll constantly be tweaking your Project as the months go on.

As we interviewed hundreds of networkers, we noticed that their Projects had similar characteristics. Most of their big-time, long-term, networking efforts could pass at least four out of the following five tests.

The Doorway Test

Ask yourself, "Who do I need to know? Who are my ideal customers, clients or employers? How do I want them to perceive me? Where will I find these people? Where do they spend time? How can I participate in their Arenas?"

Will your Strategic Positioning Project position you so that the people who can help you achieve your goal are streaming by? Find—or create—a "doorway." Put yourself in that doorway so you meet those people and they begin to know you.

Melinda, a partner in a CPA firm, had to look to find the "doorway" that would lead to her goal: a constant stream of women business owners as clients. She found someone in her network to propose her name for the Board of Directors of the Women's Business Center, whose mission is to guide and support women business owners. The Board position gave her credibility and visibility.

Melinda also taught classes at the Center on financial matters for growing businesses, whether they were start-ups or pulling in revenues of a million or more. As woman business owners became familiar with Melinda's expertise, some selected her as their CPA.

Mitch, a 28-year-old attorney, specialized in wills and trusts. When he moved to Chicago to join a firm there, he knew no one. He'd be the first to tell you that he found his Project—and his "doorway"—by accident. A guy who loved ballroom dancing, he noticed a newspaper article about a tea dance at a downtown hotel. He went to the dance and enjoyed himself hugely. The second time he attended, it hit him: The senior citizens at the dance were potential clients. Sure enough, as he got acquainted with his dancing partners, they naturally asked about his work and enough of them eventually became clients that the partners sat up and took notice.

To pass The Doorway Test, make sure your Project puts you in your target's doors or brings them to yours.

The All or Nothing Test

If people see you doing one thing well, they will assume that you are good at everything. If people see you doing one thing poorly, they will assume that you do nothing well. That's the All or Nothing Rule. Is your Strategic Positioning Project a vehicle for demonstrating your Character and Competence? Even if your networking activity has nothing to do with your exact area of career expertise, people just naturally make the leap that you must be good at your job—if you are Competent—as you perform your networking activity.

Evan wanted to become known to government human resources professionals who could hire the trainers and consultants his firm placed. Over many years, he became active in The Training Officers

> **Your Project will make you the natur and only choice.**

Conference, a professional group that meets monthly and has an annual conference. He showcased his approach to training and development in a luncheon speech he gave for the group called "Change Reaction and the Power of New Ideas." He became known to others by working on the Awards Committee. He soaked up information on trends and challenges from the many professional development programs he attended and from the conversations he had with contacts. He looked for ways to support other members and funnel good information to them. He established his Character and Competence. His long-term commitment to the well-being of the group and the people he meets there has often made his firm the natural and only choice when training and consulting are needed.

Lee's goal is to look for a satisfying, part-time retirement career. As a tax attorney, he had developed a reputation for being able to explain hard-to-understand concepts. Through his network, he was asked to teach in an executive MBA program. Teaching was a natural for him. Student evaluations tipped Lee off that storytelling was his strong suit. Lee created a Project to investigate storytelling as his next career. He used his network to find a speech coach and to discover the best storytelling festivals and workshops to attend.

To pass The All or Nothing Test, be sure your Project gives you places to showcase your abilities. Then, perform brilliantly. That way, you'll get a reputation for doing everything well.

The Bottom-Line Test

Can you arrange the time in your schedule and the money in your budget to support your Strategic Positioning Project? Will your networking efforts take you one step forward toward your goal?

Louisa is a financial planner whose long-term goal is to be invited to give a two-minute "financial tip" for women every day on CNN. To prepare for that opportunity, she found a networking contact to propose her as host for a monthly show for women to her local cable TV station. She's developed a circle of contacts at the station and is learning from them everything she'll need to know to be comfortable in the world of TV. Louisa estimates that the Project will cost her about $5,000 this year and take about three days a month. That's a huge investment, but she's confident that the experience she's gaining with her show will lead to a syndicated show and ultimately that call from CNN.

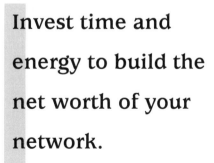

Invest time and energy to build the net worth of your network.

Dan's goal as a human resources manager is to make an extraordinary contribution at work. He's in charge of the corporation's

Employee Satisfaction Survey. After talking with several trusted colleagues, he decided that his Strategic Positioning Project should be to join The Horizon Group, made up of people from other Fortune 500 companies who have the same responsibility. He knew that membership would help him and his company learn state-of-the-art survey strategies. To prompt an invitation to this exclusive group, he networked with several Horizon Group members he knew. When he was invited to join, Dan then had to convince his boss that budgeting for the Horizon Group's weeklong annual conference and the $5,000 membership fee would be worth it. He made a detailed proposal that was accepted, even in a year when money was tight.

Three months after Dan attended his first meeting, he proved to his boss the value of his Horizon Group networking Project. He had access to survey questions that had been vetted by experts, had contacts to ask for advice on how to adapt the survey when his company acquired a German subsidiary, and he had new ideas about how to announce the results of the survey for maximum impact. Dan was nominated for an Employee-of-the-Year award and was satisfied that he and his SPP were making—and would be able to continue to make—a major contribution to his organization's success.

To pass The Bottom-Line Test, make sure you are spending your time and money in the best way to reach your goal. Put together a Strategic Positioning Project with a big impact.

The Five-Year Test

Does your Strategic Positioning Project set the stage for the phone call you want to receive in three to five years?

Deirdre has had jobs of increasing responsibility in the high-tech industry. She accepted a job offer from a company she really wanted to work for even though it was a lateral move. Not content to languish too long in this mid-level marketing position, she designed a Strategic Positioning Project. Her goal? To become known to people in the corporate hierarchy who might tap her unused talents and advocate for her when openings come up. She made a list of the folks she especially wanted to know—and to know her. She used her job as program chair for her professional development association to take the first step. When her committee decided to do a program on Employee Retention Strategies, Deirdre invited one of the people on her list, her second-level manager, to be on the panel. Deirdre had several opportunities to talk with the manager before the program and to show her Character and Competence as she handled all the planning details. She even offered to drive her manager to and from the event because parking was difficult and because, of course, she knew they'd have more time to talk.

To pass The Five-Year Test, be sure every activity in your Project helps to create the outcome you want down the road.

The Pig in Mud Test

Does your Project represent a magnificent blend of your unique personal and professional interests? Does it represent who you are, what you value, what you like to do, where you want to go, and what you do best? Will your Project make you as happy as a pig in mud? We are from Kansas, and we have seen pigs in mud. They wallow. They roll. They close their eyes in ecstasy. They are happy, content, comfortable, and want to be right where they are and no place else.

Morris, owner of a mortgage company, graduated from the university 15 years ago. An active alumni and avid supporter of the university's basketball team, he had a strong network of contacts in the university's alumni association. He created a Project that helped his alma mater, allowed him expand his business in a very natural way, and made him very happy. Here's how it happened. It came to his attention that the president of the university didn't have any discretionary funds to use for worthy projects that came up from time to time. So Morris offered to start the President's Club. Through networking, Morris assembled a group of generous donors who created a fund for the President to use on innovative projects that would improve the University's visibility and attract talented students. When students wanted to enter a robotics contest in Japan, they were able to buy their supplies and their airline tickets with money from the fund. Imagine how the President bragged about his students when they won the contest, and how grateful he was to Morris for creating the fund!

In his nationwide fundraising campaign, Morris found that alums often asked about his business and some wanted him to handle their mortgages. Morris expanded his business so that he could do mortgages in many states and took his business to a whole new level.

When Jeanne decided that she wanted to find the "capstone job" of her career, she made a list of thirty-eight people in the non-profit area. Her plan? Talk with these folks as a way to survey what's going on in philanthropy. She'd call and ask them to lunch "to explore what's next in our career field." She went into these conversations with two goals: connecting and learning. Notice that job-hunting was not her primary goal. She had a job that she could stay in until she found that ideal position. "I'm Irish. The best fun in the world to me is talking and brainstorming with people," she says. "And our conversations were always two sided—their career and my career." After thirty-two conversations—over almost a year—she got the call she wanted. When she picked up the phone, one of her contacts said, "There's a new job here that I want to tell you about. We had you in mind when we wrote the job description for this new position." It was perfect.

To pass The Pig in Mud Test, be sure your Project makes you happy!

Bonus: Get Off to a Good Start

1. Get specific about your goal. Write it down in detail.

2. Determine what size networking Project your goal demands.

3. Decide how much time and money you are going to commit to your Project.

4. Check these figures against the time and money you spent during the past 12 months. See any difference? What are the implications as you plan your Project?

5. Analyze the chart you made of the Arenas you are currently involved with and decide if you want to continue your participation, make your participation more strategic, or discontinue your participation.

6. Think what you could do in your current Arenas to move toward your goal.

7. If you decide you need to find new Arenas, make some notes about what you will be looking for.

8. Do you need help conceptualizing your Project? Decide if you want to ask individuals (Who?) for suggestions, put together a brainstorming group (Who?), look for models (Where?). Read all of this book for ideas.

9. Think about what research you'll need to do to figure out the right networking activities for your Project.

10. Begin to keep a list of your networking options.

11. Start talking about your goal and networking Project. This will do two things: help you clarify your Project and help you gather good ideas.

12. Decide if your plans so far will help you pass The Doorway Test and put you in touch with the people you need to meet.

13. Figure out if your plans so far will help you pass The All or Nothing Test and allow you to show your Character and Competence.

14. Do all of your plans so far pass The Bottom-Line Test? Can you spend the necessary time and money? And do the activities you have in mind clearly take you toward your goal? Are there peripheral or extraneous activities that you could cut to streamline your Project?

15. Can you see how doing this Project will result in your eventually getting the phone call you want or creating the opportunity that will signal you've reached your goal? Does your Project pass The Five Test?

16. Does the thought of forging ahead with your Project make you happy? Does it pass The Pig in Mud Test and blend your personal and professional interests?

17. As you plan and implement your networking Project, are you ready to learn everything you can about networking from this book?

We encourage you to start right now. We'll be cheering you on every step of the way to your goal.

PART III

Sharpen Your Skills

You say you weren't born with the gift of gab? That's okay. Anyone can learn how to turn small talk into smart talk. Here you'll discover state-of-the-art skills and secrets nobody ever told you about—the rules and tools that make networking easy. Whether you think of yourself as out-going and gregarious, or shy and retiring, you'll be able to enter a roomful of strangers enthusiastically, comfortably, and professionally. Worried that you don't know the no-nos? Take a look at the Top Twenty Turn-Offs, things no savvy networker would ever be caught dead doing.

What really happens when you meet someone? Do you muddle through those oh-so-important first few minutes? We'll help you rid yourself of the worn-out rituals that don't work. And you'll find out exactly what to say and do to manage those three Million-Dollar Moments that happen over and over again every time you shake hands. You'll learn how to get the most out of every conversation from "Hello" to "Good-bye." Want to know what to do next to enlist the people you meet in your network? You'll discover many ways to reconnect, stay in touch, and follow up.

CHAPTER 6

Know the "Netiquette"

Do you wonder, "What's the right thing to do?" If you know the networking protocols, you'll never be at a loss. You'll be able to put your best foot forward, in every networking moment.

Enter Enthusiastically

For many people, the hardest part of networking isn't talking at all; it's entering a room full of strangers. Your Critic may be saying, "Everybody knows each other but me. Everybody's better at this than I am. Everybody's looking at me." Nonsense. That's just not so. "I enter a room in an upbeat way with a smile," says Martha. "That way people want to talk with me. Sometimes people coming into a room look so serious and forbidding that they give signals that say, 'Don't talk to me!' I like to let my body language show that I'm glad I'm here."

That's good advice. Often, people spend a lot of time before an event fussing with their hair, their clothes, their makeup. Of course, you'll want to look your best. But be sure, also, to put on a smile and energize yourself. The way you relate to space sends a message. The pace of your entry and the amount of space you take up indicate your level of confidence. If you move slowly, edge into the room keeping your back to the wall, and make little or no eye contact with people, you will look uncomfortable. Relax. To energize yourself, listen to your Coach's encouragement. (For more about your Coach, see Chapter 2.) Talk to yourself. Use positive statements like:

▶ "This is going to be interesting."

▶ "I'm ready and eager to talk to people today."

▶ "I wonder what great ideas and opportunities I can discover as I talk with these people."

Brighten Up Your Body Language

What messages are you sending through your body language? As you talk with someone, you either provide "rewards," through your positive responses, or "punishments," through your lack of response or negative responses. If you are providing rewards, people will enjoy talking with you. If you provide only punishments, they'll move on to someone else. Look at Figure 6-1 for non-verbal cues to know.

FIGURE 6-1. Non-Verbal Cues.

To Encourage	To Discourage
Keep eye contact for seven to eight seconds before looking away.	Look away frequently, especially at new people entering the room.
Lean forward.	Lean or move away.
Keep your body facing your partner.	Turn your body away so that you are standing shoulder-to-shoulder, rather than face-to-face.
React to your partner by nodding and smiling.	Keep a poker face.

ENGAGE Your Partner

Use your body language to reward and encourage your partner in conversation. The letters ENGAGE can help you remember how to give a positive message through your body language as you talk with people.

E = **Establishing Eye Contact.** If you're looking anywhere on your partner's face, she will feel that you are looking her in the eye. In our culture, we break eye contact every seven or eight seconds or so. Glance away and then back. It's more flattering to your partner to glance down to the side and then back at your partner's face rather than over her shoulder, as if you are looking for someone else to talk with.

N = Nodding. Nod to show that you're following and enjoying the conversation.

G = Geniality. Be cheerful and cordial. Your geniality tells your partner that you're having fun in the conversation. Smile. Do it often, but appropriately. Nervousness can lead to smiling at serious or even sad topics. Women who are concerned about being perceived as assertive should be careful to smile only when the occasion or topic warrants.

A = Aiming Your Attention. Let your body language acknowledge that your full attention is concentrated on your partner. Lean slightly forward.

G = Gesturing Appropriately. Use your hands to emphasize key words or concepts. Watch other people to expand your use of gestures. The people who are the most comfortable will use more expansive motions. But small gestures work well in close-up conversation, too.

E = Easing Your Posture. Stand comfortably, with your feet slightly apart and your back straight. Center your weight so that you don't sway or feel off-balance.

In a crowded, noisy room, you can create a "bubble" for you and your conversational partner with your eye contact, your gestures, and your forward-leaning posture.

Tune Up Your Tone of Voice

Do you sound whiny? Tentative? Bored? Do you sound like a schoolmarm? A drill sergeant? A mouse? A judge? How do you want to sound? What tone of voice would support you as you present yourself?

Read a couple of children's books into a tape recorder. Try to really "be" the characters and create different voices for each of them. This exercise has several benefits: You widen your range of available "voices," you find out how you sound, and when you have finished analyzing your tape, you have a nice present to give to a child you know!

You also might tape yourself in various situations, such as at the office or at the dinner table. If you just turn on the recorder and let it run, you'll eventually forget about it and record your voice in its "natural" state.

Make your voice sound more confident and energetic. If your voice sounds too high, deepen it. Move it down the scale one whole tone. If you sound draggy and tired, speed up your delivery. Radio announcers read about 150 words a minute. Moving along a bit faster than that will make you more interesting to listen to. If you seem to be talking in a monotone, emphasize key words by moving up or down the scale. Making some words higher or lower than the rest avoids a flat delivery and allows your energy and enthusiasm to come through. Also, increase or decrease your volume to emphasize key words.

Consider Closeness

Each culture has different "rules" about how close conversation partners should stand when they talk to one another. In the U.S., we stand about three feet apart to have social conversations. If the room is very noisy or if the conversation becomes more personal, we move in, closing the range to perhaps eighteen inches. If we move closer than that, we are usually having an intimate conversation. If your partners in conversation typically move away from you, you may be violating this "rule." On the other hand, if you talk from farther away or move away during a conversation, your partner may think of you as "stand-offish" or "distant."

Sometimes a person moves away from his conversation partner for other reasons. Television commercials for products like deodorants and mouthwash have created anxiety about being close to other people. The most sensible thing to do is to take reasonable precautions and then don't worry about these problems.

Watch What You Put in Your Mouth

In business or social situations, neither smoking nor excessive drinking is acceptable behavior.

If the event involves eating, use your best manners. At a stand-up networking meeting, choose foods that are easy to eat, such as grapes, crackers, or bits of cheese. Steer clear of the chewy, dripping, garlic-laced, hard-to-eat items at the hors d'oeuvres table. If you worry about a piece of spinach attaching itself to your front tooth or about dripping shrimp sauce on your tie, don't eat.

If the etiquette of eating concerns you, read a book on manners, find a course on etiquette in your community or encourage your organization to offer one. There's no point in letting concerns about manners sabotage your ability to be at ease with people.

Treat Touching as Taboo

Except for shaking hands, it's usually inappropriate in business settings to touch your partner. Two people of the same gender and "rank," however, may be comfortable touching during a conversation. In general, though, it's either the female or the more powerful person who initiates touching during a conversation. If a woman touches, it may be interpreted as flirting. If a person of higher "rank" touches, it may be an indication to his partner that he or she is pulling rank, trying to establish control, or even engaging in sexual harassment.

Unless you have established a special relationship with someone in which touching is acceptable, don't do it. And even if you have a warm relationship with someone—especially someone of the opposite sex—it's better to err on the side of formality in public.

Forego Flirting

Marilyn says, "As a woman, I'm concerned that people will misinterpret my friendliness. I don't want them to think I'm flirting."

Jorge says, "I worry about the Dos and Don'ts of networking with women."

Those worries are unnecessary if you're clear about the difference between flirting and networking and if you "read" the unwritten ground rules in different organizational cultures. For example, two past presidents of one professional organization—in this case, a man and a woman who have known each other for nearly two decades—hug when they meet. In other groups, that behavior might be off-limits.

In business situations, you'll want to avoid a sexual come-on. If you know how to flirt, then you can figure out how not to. But just in case you do it unconsciously, take a look at some common flirting behaviors.

Men flirt by extending eye contact beyond the normal length of time (more than eight seconds or so), which signals attention and interest. A man also may indicate a romantic interest by inappropriate or extended touching, a handshake that turns into a hand holding, for example. Or he may sit closer than necessary. Or he may assume responsibility for a woman's comfort through excessively solicitous hovering. It is not appropriate in a business setting for a man to open doors, help remove a woman's coat or pull out her chair. Or rather, it's not appropriate if the behavior is unilateral. If either party helpfully opens a door for the other person, who is encumbered, that's fine. A man doesn't need to offer to carry packages or suitcases. He shouldn't use a diminutive nickname —saying Katie for Kathryn, for example. If a man introduces himself as William, you'll *never* hear a woman say, "Hi, Billy." That's a put-down in business. So are overly enthusiastic comments about a woman's dress or hair or other personal compliments beyond, "You're looking well."

Women flirt using many of the same tactics. Eye contact, especially lowering the head and looking up through the lashes, can be flirtatious. So can touching in a proprietary manner, fingering a man's tie, for example, or brushing lint off his shoulder. Women also flirt by touching their own hair or twisting a curl. They might stand closer than normal. Inappropriate laughter is another clue. So is calling a man "honey" or "love." Women might "serve" men, offering to bring them coffee, for example. Most comments about a man's clothing or hair are also off-limits.

None of these behaviors is appropriate in a business context.

Pay Your Way

By the way, always pay your fair share of the cost of networking. It's better to go "dutch treat" than to pay for a networking contact's meals, for example. Remember, you're trying to establish a mutually beneficial relationship. Ignore titles, and work on developing peer relationships, not superior-subordinate relationships. If one person always pays, the relationship also will become unequal. You can't buy a networking contact. Most relationships work best when each person pays his or her way, not only with money, but also with valuable information or referrals or resources.

Exchange Business Cards Effectively

Handing a business card to someone does not constitute a networking relationship. Strangely enough, the biggest mistake people make with business cards is giving them out too freely, too soon. When that happens, your contact will go back to the office, look at the card, say to himself, "I wonder who this is?" and throw the card in the wastebasket.

Challenge yourself not to give your card out until you've found some connection, some reason for exchanging names and phone numbers. Approach conversations asking yourself, "I wonder what she needs that I can provide? Let's see if I can figure it out," and "I know what I'm looking for today. Wonder if I can find someone who has the information I need?"

Handing out your business card makes only a "cardboard connection."

You have to work to make a conversation lead to the exchange of cards. When you hit upon a reason to trade cards, you have accomplished something very important. You have extended the relationship beyond the event at which you met.

Jewell mentioned her aerobics class to Tess, a woman she met at a seminar. Tess mentioned that she wanted to find a low-cost exercise program, so Jewell asked for her card and said she'd send some information. The next time Jewell went to her aerobics class, she picked up a catalog from Parks and Recreation, took it home, and mailed it to Tess.

When you find a conversational connection and need to exchange cards, take a moment right then and there—or as soon as you leave the event—to note on the back of the card anything you want to remember about the person, the conversation, or what you agreed to do: "Has twins." "Went to Duke University." "Wants to know more about the Chamber of Commerce networking night."

"Needs speaker." If you have promised to do something, follow through.

The next time you see your contact, you don't have to start all over again. You can build on the information that you provided. You might update your contact on how you are using the information he sent you: "Thanks so much for sending me Tom's phone number. He sounds like just the speaker we need for our sales meeting. We plan to meet next week."

If someone gives you her card the moment you meet, don't just stuff it in your pocket. Read it carefully. Use it as a visual aid. Look at her name and learn it. Discuss her title. Notice the organization. Ask about it. If it's an engineering firm, ask what kinds of engineering projects it specializes in.

> **Tickle yourself. Jot reminders on the backs of cards you collect, so that you can follow up and follow through.**

Then give her your card and use it as an aid to teach her about you. "My card says Robert James Hensy, but everybody calls me 'R.J.' My office is about five blocks from yours at Tenth and Broad. I've listed some of the health care management services my firm provides on the back of my card. Our new facility is for patients with Alzheimer's. Did you see the story about it in the Kansas City Star last Sunday?"

Join Groups Comfortably

In any room full of people, most people will be talking in groups. You certainly can look around to find someone else who is not attached to a group and make a beeline for that person. Barbara says, "When I feel nervous about joining a group, I form my own. I look for someone standing alone and start a conversation with that person."

Or you can join a group. In our workshops, people ask, "How can I break into a group?" We tease them a bit: "Well, first, you find a big sledgehammer. . . ." We choose not to use the phrase "break into a group." Breaking in implies that you must force yourself on the group, a violent act; joining implies that the group was incomplete without you!

To join in, signal that you're committed to becoming part of the conversation. Gently but firmly touch the arm of one person. Almost always, the circle will open up to allow you to come on in. Don't be tentative; show commitment by making eye contact with the speaker or smiling at one of the listeners. Take a few seconds to listen. You can start participating any time you feel tuned in to what's going on. When the conversation slows, turn to a person next to you and introduce yourself. Often, someone else in the group will initiate introductions. If people in the group seem to be acquainted, ask, "How do you all know each other?" as a way to prompt introductions.

If someone quickly introduces everyone in the group to you, don't despair. Simply go back to each individual later and say, "Let's introduce ourselves again. It's hard to catch everyone's name in a group."

If joining a group is uncomfortable for you, analyze why. Are you remembering high school? Most of us have vivid memories of feeling excluded—even people who were members of an "ingroup." As grown-ups, we still carry some of those adolescent feelings around with us. Analyze what your Critic says when you think about joining a group. When you bring the Critic's comments out into the light of day and examine them, they usually will seem quite ridiculous and based on leftover angst from your teenage years:

▶ "They don't want to talk to me."

▶ "They are talking about me."

▶ "They don't want to include me."

▶ "They will laugh at me or tell me to go away."

When a new person joins your group, smile, nod, and make eye contact. When whoever is talking comes to a stopping point, fill the newcomer in. Say, "Jack was just telling us about his new job." Then look back at Jack so he can continue.

Sometimes people worry that they might be joining a private or intimate conversation. Trust your powers of observation. You will be able to tell when a private conversation is taking place. Here are some clues. People may be touching. There may be visible emotion. Voices may be very low or higher than normal. They may move closer to each other.

If you enter a conversation that's too intimate, or if you don't like the topic, you can leave comfortably. If the conversation is too personal, say, "Looks like I've interrupted something. I'll talk with you later." Or, "This feels like a private conversation. I'll catch you later." Or, if the topic is not something you want to talk about, say, "Hey, I'll talk with you later. It looks like you're really getting into this topic." You may find that one of the people who's involved in the intimate conversation or talking about the topic you're trying to avoid will regard you as a savior and welcome you into the group as an excuse to reduce the level of intimacy or change the topic.

If you're still unsure about how to present yourself with greater confidence, ask yourself, "How would I act if I had just 10 percent more confidence? Or 25 percent more? Or 50 percent more?" Then act that way.

Bonus: Ten Tips on the Nuances of "Netiquette"

Whether you are at a networking event or a ball game, keep these tips in mind to be comfortable and professional as you make contact.

1. Be polite, positive and politic. Don't ask, "Has your boss calmed down any?" Ask, "How's morale in your office these days?" Don't ask, "Have the lay-offs finally stopped at your company?" Ask, "Are things back to normal at your company?"

2. Check in with acquaintances. Meeting new people may actually be easier than beginning a conversation with a person you see only rarely and know only slightly. Don't berate yourself for not remembering all the details of that person's life or work. And, it's easy to put your foot in your mouth inadvertently when you begin a conversation with someone you haven't talked with recently. Assume that the person's life has changed. It probably has.

"A man I'd worked with several years ago had transferred to another division of the company," says Jerry. "Seeing him again, I asked about his wife. He said, 'Oh, we've been divorced for two years.'" To avoid that kind of slip-up, ask general questions rather than specific ones. "We haven't talked for a while. Catch me up on what you're doing." "How's your year been?" "What's changed for you since we've talked?" "What's new in your life?" These kinds of questions allow the other person to bring you up to date, revealing as much as he wishes. The answers will guide your conversation.

3. Go for the relationship, not the contract. When you meet casually, and the conversation moves to a "let's do some business" level, set up a convenient time to call or place to meet to complete the transaction. As you continue to talk in the casual meeting, build your relationship with your contact. If you swap stories about trout fishing with a new acquaintance and develop a strong rapport, he's more likely to think of you when he needs an accountant than if you spend most of the conversation aggressively pushing your accounting services.

4. Relationships that bounce back and forth from friendship to selling are tricky, no doubt about it. Be scrupulously honest about your intentions to keep the boundaries clear and avoid abusing a friend's trust.

> Go for the relationship, not the contract.

Nora and Lee had known each other for fifteen years. Lee's job was eliminated, and she went into business for herself. Nora, the marketing director for a law firm, called Lee and asked her to recommend a computer software trainer. More than a year later, after the two had visited at several professional meetings, Lee called Nora and set up a lunch meeting, saying, "I want to hear about the condo you are building and catch up with your life. I also want to tell you about a series of seminars I just finished doing for employees at the bank. I think your organization might find these seminars useful." Lee made her Agenda clear as she was issuing the invitation. Their lunch conversation ranged from personal items to the seminar series, and Nora asked for additional information about the seminars so she could consider them for her employees.

5. Make judicial choices about what parts of your personal life you are willing to talk about in networking situations. Mae, an attor-

ney with a mid-sized firm, is building a reputation for being a fascinating person to talk to—about a lot of things. Even though adoption law isn't her specialty, she has two adopted children, so she shares what she knows and then refers prospective parents to an attorney with many years of experience in that field. She also is a stand-up comic. She is careful about bringing her passion for comedy into the conversation because she doesn't want it to affect people's perception of her as a lawyer.

6. Notice people. You may think it's not proper to ask about his tan or her beautiful necklace. Why not? As children, we may have asked embarrassing questions about the obvious ("Why is Aunt Betty's tummy so fat?") and been shushed rather than told she was pregnant. As children, we may have gotten another message, a far deeper one: "Don't notice other people." In school, teachers said, "Keep your eyes on your own paper." Other adults may have told us, "It's not polite to make personal remarks." Comedian Lenny Bruce once said, "When you are eight years old, nothing is any of your business." Some of the rules we were taught as children no longer apply.

"Before a business meeting got underway," Meg remembers, "I joined a group of three or four people who were chatting. One of them, John, had his arm in a cast. I figured the rest of the group had already asked him, 'What happened?' So I decided not to ask again. As the meeting started, I asked Betty what happened to John's arm. She said, 'Oh, I don't know. Nobody asked about that.'"

7. Make talking to you easy, not hard. Don't put yourself down. You will discourage conversation if you say, "I'm just a secretary." Or, "I'm just a housewife." After one of those statements, your conversation partner is at a loss for what to talk with you about. If you are feeling like an underdog in a situation, be sure you are prepared to talk about something interesting. See Chapter 10 for ideas.

8. Edit the jargon from your conversation. If you say, "I'm the EXO for the DDG," you'll stop the conversation cold. If you are talking with people outside your company and occupation, be sure you translate any specialized language into terms that anyone can understand.

9. Be on the lookout for role models. When you find someone who handles situations in a way that you'd like to, observe how they do it. It's all right to copy someone else's manner. Do it consistently, and it will become part of your own style.

10. Just say "Hi!" What's the most successful opener for starting a conversation with somebody? There's nothing complicated about the answer. The word is "Hi!" Just "Hi!"

It's a "Hi!" that flashes a message in neon lights: "I feel great about meeting you, and I'd like to talk with you." That "Hi!" says, "I'm happy to be here, and I'm looking forward to getting to know you." It's inviting and energizing and relaxing at the same time. It's inviting and energizing because it signals that you're a person who is committed to helping this conversation move along. It's relaxing because it signals that you're a person who can take care of himself in a conversation. It's not the kind of "Hi" that sends the message, "I'm just saying this to be polite, and I hope you won't take this as a signal that we have to talk." What a difference! And the difference comes from the tone of voice and the body language. Practice the two kinds of "Hi!" Feel the difference between the two.

Joan remembers learning about the power of just saying "Hi". "Shortly after I was married I went downtown for lunch with a neighbor, whose name was Sue Jones," she says. "We went to the department store cafeteria. You could sit anywhere. We went over to a table and put our trays down. Sue looked at the two strangers sitting there and said, 'Hi, I'm Sue Jones.' I never would have introduced myself to strangers. I was so stunned, so impressed. So, I made a button in my brain and labeled it Sue Jones. After that, when I would go to various events, I would push my button and say, 'Hi, I'm Joan Martinson.' That helped me to begin talking— just pretending I was Sue. I still do it. I still, ten years later, have my Sue Jones button. When I'm uncomfortable being myself or when I'm feeling shy, I push the button, become Sue Jones, and I'm immediately comfortable reaching out to people."

Talk to strangers. Take every opportunity to meet someone new.

CHAPTER 7

Avoid the Top Twenty Turn-Offs

Do some networkers drive you crazy or display an appalling lack of "netiquette?" It's easy to recognize other people's "sins," the things that turn you off. Of course you wouldn't commit any of these faux pas, would you? You'll be a more attractive conversational partner if you avoid these twenty turn-offs.

1. **Don't tell all the details.** The classic definition of a bore is someone who, when you ask him how he is, tells you. The person who insists on telling everything will soon lose his audience. Ever notice how infuriating it is to listen to someone who wonders out loud, "Let's see, was it Tuesday or Wednesday?" Who cares? Get on with the story. Don't include everything; sketch in the broad outlines. Follow the tips in Chapter 11 for telling brisk, compelling Success Stories about your experiences.

2. **Don't do monologues and interrupt others**. This bore never lets you get a word in edgewise. He trounces your comments with non-stop verbiage of his own. Hogging the airtime, he insists on having the first, the middle, and the last word. He especially likes to interrupt subordinates and women to show who's more powerful. He ignores questions and insists on directing the conversation himself. Encourage and invite others to participate. If they don't leap in,

79

ask them a question and wait for their answer. See Chapter 11 for ideas on turning monologues into dialogues.

3. *Don't interrogate people.* Persistence is usually counted as a virtue. However, you have to know when to stop pushing and probing. The interrogator doesn't. Long after a topic has run out of steam, the interrogator is still battering his conversational partner. Tone of voice has as much to do with interrogation as the wording of questions or comments. They are delivered in an accusatory tone, often belittling or demeaning to his partner. He says, "You should. . . ." It's one of his favorite phrases. "Why don't you . . . ?" runs a close second. "Surely you know that. . . ." ranks right up there. The interrogator generally has strong feelings about the topic and pushes his partner for agreement. State your ideas but don't try to convert others to your way of thinking or push your opinions down their throats. If an interrogator puts you on the spot, say, "Why on earth would you ask me about that? I never talk about. . . ." Or, "Are you comfortable talking about that? I'm not." Depersonalize the topic. Move the question from one that makes you uncomfortable to a topic you'd like to discuss.

4. *Don't insist on one-upmanship.* The person who always has a better story than yours or a better deal to crow about is committing one-upmanship. She can never merely accept a comment or story; she has to top it with one of her own. These people use conversation to make themselves look wonderful—sometimes at the expense of others. If you've closed a $1 million deal, they've got a $5 million one to tell about. If you went skiing at Keystone, they went to the Alps. Don't play the "Can You Top This?" game.

5. *Don't seek free advice.* This person wants something for nothing. He corners doctors to ask about his physical symptoms, lawyers to ask about planning his estate, computer consultants for detailed advice on updating his firewall. He abuses his partners by asking them questions in a networking situation that he should be asking in a more formal situation. Don't ask for free professional advice when you should be paying for it.

6. *Don't hide.* Some people, not wanting to appear self-centered, never tell you anything about themselves. You have to pry it out of them. Or they downplay what they have done, leaving you to feel quite foolish when you discover, through additional questions or other means, what it is they are obliquely referring to. If you bring up a topic, be sure it's one that you feel comfortable discussing fully.

7. *Don't be dogmatic*. These people have all the answers and merely want to make converts to their way of thinking. They want confirmation of what they've already decided. Compare them to listeners who keep an open mind to gain understanding and sometimes, as a result of talking with others, even change their point of view. People do expect to be comfortable as they network. They don't want to be harangued by someone who is trying to change their mind or force opinions down their throats.

8. *Don't give unsolicited advice.* If you evaluate your own life, you reveal yourself—not a bad thing to do in conversation. But, if you evaluate others' lives, you may offend them. Know the difference. Never say, "Why don't you . . . ?" Or even worse, "You should. . . ." Or "You should have. . . ." If you feel that your experience might be helpful to someone else, ask permission. Say, "Would you like to hear about what I did in that kind of situation?"

9. *Don't be a bigot.* Unfortunately, bigots come in many varieties. These are the people who make ethnic, religious, or sexual comments to put down others. Bigots insult various people in various ways. They stereotype, lumping people into groups and making comments about that group as if those comments apply equally to all. They generalize based on a single experience or a small number of experiences. Or they tell jokes that play off stereotypes. In any form, bigotry is highly offensive and exhibiting it discourages others from trusting you. If someone makes a bigoted remark, practice your assertive behavior. Force him to examine his prejudices. Call attention to them. A hearty executive grabbed a woman's hand at a meeting saying "You must be Marvin's secretary!" The woman calmly replied, "Why would you think I'm someone's secretary?" It may be necessary to keep the bigot's good will and to help him save face. If so, speak in a light tone of voice. Tact is the knack of making a point without making an enemy.

> **People expect to be comfortable as they network.**

10. *Don't whine.* Whiners never have anything good to say. They go on and on about their health (Dreadful!), the economy (Dreadful!), today's teenagers (Dreadful!). You know the type. What a downer! Don't allow yourself to be perceived as a whiner.

11. *Don't do hard sells.* When Benny goes to a networking event, he thinks he should get somebody's name on a contract right then and there. He walks up to people and says, "Hi, I'm Benny. I sell specialty advertising items. I could make your business card into a refrigerator magnet and have it ready for you by next week." Contrary to what many people think, a networking event is not a place to sell. It's a place to make contact with people so that you can arrange to meet them later to do business. Benny isn't focusing on building trust; he's putting all his energy into finding a customer. He needs to back off and cultivate the relationship. That's when he'll begin to attract clients.

Networking events are places to make plans to get togethe later.

12. *Don't assume you will get paid.* Gina gave Carlotta the name of a potential client to call. Carlotta followed up and contacted the prospect. She got the contract and wrote Gina a note of thanks for the lead, saying that she would be on the alert for something to send Gina's way. Gina's response was to bill Carlotta for a 10 percent "finder's fee." Most networking implies reciprocity. It is okay to charge a finder's fee only if that agreement is made up front. Generally, expert networkers consider such arrangements to be self-defeating because they do not necessarily develop the relationship. They'd rather have someone looking out for an opportunity to give them. If, however, someone does something for you that results in business, and you know you'll never have an opportunity to pay her back, then you might consider paying a finder's fee or sending a gift. Thea wrote a magazine article quoting Dorothy, who lived in the Midwest, Dorothy got a call from someone who read the article. That person became a client of Dorothy's. In gratitude, Dorothy sent Thea a finder's fee.

13. *Don't make unreasonable requests.* Be careful what you ask for. Una, a part-time professor, told her class of eleven graduate students to call and interview certain middle managers in her company. The next time one of the managers saw Una, he asked her, rather pointedly, to check with him before making that kind of assignment in the future because it was too time-consuming for him to talk to so many students during his busy workday. The professor apologized and was especially careful for several months to look for ways to be helpful to all the managers to repay them for the inconvenience she had thoughtlessly caused them.

14. *Don't confuse contacts with friends.* "Networking, ugh!" says Yvonne. "I just want to be friends with people." You can develop friendships with networking contacts, but it takes time, something many business people don't have. It's possible to have many "warm" business contacts without turning them into friendships. Women are more likely than men to be confused by the invisible line that separates contacts from confidants. Don't worry about it. Be friendly with your contacts. If a friendship takes root, fine; if not, you still have a good contact.

15. *Don't abuse people's trust.* Your work may deal with sensitive information or business intelligence. Don't pass it on without careful thought. As you tell stories to illustrate your Character and Competence, disguise real situations if they are sensitive. If you are a real estate agent who sold a house that was part of a divorce settlement, for instance, you would, of course, avoid using your clients' real names. Don't give out a contact's name or use one person's name to make contact with another person unless you ask permission first. The world is a small place, and word gets around if you violate someone's confidence. Always be trustworthy.

16. *Don't be so eager to provide resources that you pass along names of people or organizations that you haven't thoroughly checked out.* Before you give your contact a name, be sure that person's or organization's performance will reflect well on you. Jon asked Charlie if he knew of a good foundation repair company. Jon, wanting to be helpful, told him the name of the contractor who was working on his neighbor's basement. Unfortunately, the neighbor, unbeknownst to Jon, had just filed suit against the contractor.

17. *Don't burden others with inappropriate or intimate information.* You have to know someone very well before it's appropriate to discuss your daughter's divorce or how much you spent on your last vacation.

18. *Don't expect to get without giving.* The absolutely worst thing you can do is to take repeatedly from a person without reciprocating by sending information, referrals, or opportunities her way.

19. *Don't refuse to play the game.* Some people are hard to talk to because they don't take "small talk" seriously. They haven't bothered to plan ahead, to think of good topics, to notice what's on their Agenda, or to collect experiences to talk about that reveal their interests, Character, and Competence. They soak up a lot, but don't contribute. They throw all the burden of coming up with things to talk about on their conversation partners' shoulders. And heaven forbid they should ask a question or demonstrate any interest in your life! You should be ready to fully participate in the conversation.

> Anybody can learn t make small talk anc to use small talk to create valuable networking relationships.

20. *Don't forget to enjoy the journey.* It's easy to keep your eyes on the horizon—on your business goals—and fail to enjoy the ride. Sure, you're looking for business or career benefits, but relax. Take time to appreciate people's unique gifts beyond their usefulness to you at the moment. Allow yourself to enjoy encountering the unexpected. Just as you might drive around the bend and discover a wonderful view, a conversation may veer off, and you'll find you're talking about something you haven't even thought about for years or something that changes your view

> Networking is a journey, not a destination. Enjoy tl trip.

of the world. People who enjoy window-shopping or browsing through a bookstore or antique shop can get the same kick out of being with people. People take courses in art appreciation; networking can be a "course" in the appreciation of people and of life. Be ready to be delighted.

CHAPTER 8

"Who Are You?"

There are Three Big Questions that always come up in every networking encounter:

1. "Who are you?"

2. "What do you do?"

3. "What are we going to talk about?"

These questions are "Million-Dollar Moments." As you deal with them, you can either begin a relationship that might be worth who knows how much over a lifetime. Or you can muddle through these moments, relying on the worn-out rituals we all know so well for meeting and greeting. If you learn how to maximize these moments, you can make sure your business relationships start off in the best possible way.

This chapter will help you deal with the first question, "Who are you?" Learning names ranks as the Number One concern for people in our workshops: 97 percent of participants say they have trouble with this important skill. The good news is that you can learn to remember names and make yours memorable, too.

Why Remembering Names Is Hard

Okay. You're right. When people meet, they rarely say to one another, "Who are you?" What exactly do they do?

One person takes the initiative and sticks out her hand, saying, "Hi, I'm Jennifer Allsgood."

Shaking her hand, the other person responds, "Rob Schafer. Nice to meet you." "You too," says Jennifer.

How long does that name exchange take, do you suppose? In our workshops, people are amazed when they count how many seconds an introduction takes— three or four! No wonder people have trouble remembering names! You are asking the impossible of yourself to think that you can learn someone's name—and teach that person your name—in only a few seconds. Notice, too, that if you think of this moment as teaching and learning, not just saying and hearing, you'll be recognizing this moment's true importance.

> The average name exchange takes less than five seconds. N wonder we can't remember people's names!

What's the rush?

People say, "I just whiz through the name thing so I can move on to the good stuff." But in networking, names are "the good stuff." It will be mighty difficult for you to initiate a relationship with someone if you don't know that person's name. So, slow down and linger longer over the name exchange.

Learn Someone's Name

When someone says her name, do not immediately reply with your own. Instead, focus initially on learning hers.

Here are three things you can do. These ideas are so simple you may be tempted to dismiss them. Don't do that! Practice so that you can use them every time you meet someone. They work.

1. *Repeat the first name.* Say, "It's nice to meet you, Jennifer." You may think that you habitually do that, but our research indicates that less than 25 percent of people involved in introductions repeat the name. Train yourself to do it

> To remember a nam use it immediately.

every time. Hang on to the name in order to introduce Jennifer to at least one other person at that event. Whether you make that introduction thirty minutes later or three hours later, Jennifer will appreciate that you bothered to remember her name. Notice that you are focusing only on the first name. That's fine. It's the tried and true principle of "divide and conquer." Learn the person's first name first.

2. *Ask for the last name again or confirm it*. Say, "And your last name was . . .?" Or, "Tell me your last name again." Or, "And your last name is Allsgood?" The person will repeat her last name: "It's Allsgood." Or say, "Yes, it's Allsgood." Usually, people will say their last names very distinctly when you ask only for the surname. One problem with the old ritual is that people are so used to saying their names that they say them too quickly, crunching their first and last names together. When you ask specifically for the last name, your partner will say her last name clearly.

3. *Ask a question or make a comment about the person's name.* Comment either on the first name or the last name. It's a chance for you to say the name again. Here are some suggestions.

▶ "Do you like to be called Jenny or Jennifer?"

▶ "Allsgood sounds like it might be an English name. Do you know where it came from?"

Teach Your Name

Notice that you have not yet said your own name! Now is the time to do just that. Be ready to help someone learn your name. There are three things you can do.

1. *Give 'em a double dip*. Say your first name twice. "I'm Rob, Rob . . . Shafer."

2. *Separate and articulate.* Say your first and last name with a tiny pause in between and pronounce your last name crisply and distinctly. "I'm Rob, Rob (pause) Shafer."

3. *Make your name memorable.* Say something about your name to help the person you're talking with remember it. Spelling your name is a good idea because a majority of us are visual learn-

ers. We learn best when we can see the letters in our mind's eye. To help you learn her name, Jennifer might have spelled Allsgood when you asked her for it again. Nancy Mann says, "It's Mann with two 'ns.' I'm the only woman who's a Mann who's in real estate in Kansas City."

There are several concerns people have as they begin to use this system:

▶ *"It feels awkward at first."* Yes, it does. We are used to playing the Name Game like Ping Pong: Your name to me; my name back to you. That's the ritual. You'll need to practice to be comfortable with the new system because the timing is different.

▶ *"What should I do when people are wearing nametags?"* Use the nametag as a visual aid. When Bob is learning Jennifer's name, he can say, looking at the nametag, "I see your name is Jennifer. Do you ever go by a nickname?" When he is introducing himself, Bob can say, "My nametag says 'Robert,' but I prefer 'Rob.'"

▶ *"Sometimes the other person—who is still playing Ping Pong—will interrupt. What do I do then?"* Go with the flow. Answer the other person's question. Then go back to ask something else or say something else about that person's name later. The point is to talk longer about the names.

▶ *"Sometimes I'm introduced to someone and they say, 'I never can remember names.' How should I respond?"* That's your cue to say, "You can remember mine. Here's how. It's Sherry Hunter. Sherry like the drink. You can remember Hunter because I hunt down computer problems and fix them."

Try These Twenty Tips

1. Continue to use the other person's name as the conversation moves along. "Are you a new member, Fred?"

2. Look for a personal connection, perhaps someone else you know with the same name. Make the connection out loud. Tell your

partner, "Hi, Adam. Good to meet you. Adam was my college room-mate's name, so it will be easy for me to remember yours." Or, "Nice to meet you, Harriet. Wasn't your name mentioned as one of the new board members?"

3. Visualize a picture to help you remember the name. Associate the name with a picture in your mind. If you meet someone in a leadership position whose name is Arthur, visualize him as King Arthur with the Knights of the Roundtable. (Some people like this technique; others say it just confuses them. Use it if it's helpful.)

4. Ask the person to spell his or her name. "Is that Carl with a 'C' or a 'K'?" "Is that M-a-r-y or Merry as in Christmas?" If the person is wearing a nametag, you still may comment on the spelling, "I see that you spell Marsha with an 'S.'" Because most people are visual learners, seeing the letters of the name in your mind helps.

5. Ask how the person got her name. "Do you know why you were named Savannah? Were you named for the city?" We find that nearly half of our workshop participants can tell a story about how they got their names.

6. If you know something about the person, even though you've never met, mention it. Acknowledge his or her uniqueness. "I understand that this new orientation program was your idea, Kay."

7. If you notice that people often have trouble understanding your name, it may be because you are saying your name, not teaching it, and are running the two words together. This problem may be accentuated if your first name ends and your last name begins with a vowel. If your name is difficult for people to understand, separate the two names like this, "Hi, my first name is Marla; my last name is Anderson."

8. If your name comes from a culture less familiar to the people you are meeting, then you'll have to make a special effort to teach your name. Barbara Rodvani says, "Rodvani, think of a van going down a road, Rodvani." Ankur says, "It's like encore—take a bow."

9. If your last name is a hyphenated combination, say so. It's very difficult for people to understand a first name plus *two* last names. "Hi, I'm Maureen, Maureen . . . James-Martin. James is my maiden name and Martin is my husband's last name."

10. Come up with several ways to help people remember your name. As you say your name, give a little extra information so that you have a chance to repeat your name for your partner. It can be as simple as saying, "Jack's a nickname for Jackson." Or tell people where your name came from. "Stanton was my grandfather's name. I like having his name because he encouraged me to start my business." "My first name is Andreal. My mother liked the name Andrea, but she wanted something unique, so she added an 'L.'"

11. Keep your energy level high—rev it up. Let your body language and tone of voice indicate that you're seriously trying to learn your partner's name and teach your name. People say that this is very flattering.

12. Always say the person's name again as you leave to reinforce your learning. "It was good to meet you, Ronda."

13. Give yourself a realistic goal. At a networking event, for example, vow to really learn the names of five people before you leave.

14. Decide whether you want to teach your first name or your last name. If you want your contact to be able to find you in his industry directory or the phone book, concentrate on your last name. Your co-author, Anne Baber teaches both names this way: "Hi, I'm Anne, Anne Baber. It's Ann with an "e" and Babe with an "r."

15. Design a way to teach your name and what you do at the same time. Debbie, a new franchise owner does just that. She says, "Hi, I'm Debbie Danforth with Decorating Den. Just remember 'D' for Debbie and 'D' for Decorating Den."

16. If you don't like the association that people make when they hear your name, say something to redirect their attention. Even though the TV show is long gone Mindy found that people were always asking her, "Where's Mork?" So, she decided to say, "Hi, I'm Mindy, Mindy . . Jones. Mindy, like Lindy, but with an 'M.'"

17. Set up a positive association. Don't use a memory hook that links you with a negative impression. Annabel Lector used to say, "Hi, I'm Annabel Lector, like the killer in 'Silence of the Lambs.'" Now she says, "Hi, I'm Annabel Lector, like rector—an English clergyman."

18. If your name is very common, you can still make it memorable. Tom Smith says, "There are fourteen Tom Smith's in the phone book, but I'm the only one who's here tonight!" Joe Jones says, "I wish I were from Indiana so you could call me Indiana Jones. But I'm from Iowa, so call me Iowa Jones."

19. When you meet someone with a foreign-sounding name, don't assume that she is from another country. When Ying-Chie, a third-generation American, introduces herself, she often is asked, "Where are you from?" She replies, hiding her irritation, "San Francisco."

20. If your name is memorable or connects easily to some idea, you may become bored or annoyed with what people say about it. "People always say, 'Just like the bird,' when I say my name," complains Rick Robin. Find a way to use that connection. Rick, a realtor, might say, "Yes! And, as a realtor, I always find just the right nest for people!"

Break Up Bunches of Introductions

You've joined a group of people, and one of them is quickly introducing each person to you. You're thinking, "I'll never remember all these names!" What to do?

Smile. Say hello as each person is introduced. After a while, when the group breaks up, go back to each individual and introduce yourself, one-on-one, using the new system.

Deal Skillfully with Forgotten Names

Have you ever seen someone across the room and said to yourself, "I know that person. What is her name?" This is not an age-related problem; it's a brain overload problem. Let's face it, you know hundreds of people—coworkers, customers, colleagues, cousins—so the expectation that you'll never forget a name is unrealistic.

Above all, avoid the following scenario.

You see someone whose name you think you should remember across the room. You make eye contact, then hang your head, shuffle over with a discouraged look on your face, limply put out your hand and apologetically announce, "Ooooh, no! I've forgotten your name." If the person wants to make you feel better, she'll say, "Oh, I've forgotten your name too," even if she remembers it!

This low-energy start has no place to go but down as you stand around mutually beating yourselves up with a duet of, "I'm so bad with names." "No, I'm much worse." After you commiserate about how dumb you are, you finally reintroduce yourselves, all the while protesting that you'll probably forget each other again.

What should you do? You have several options. Try one of these ways to re-connect, even if you can't remember the person's name:

▶Walk up to the person, stick out your hand and say, "I remember you, I'm Craig." You're banking on the ritual. The other person will most likely say his name back.

▶If you do recall the situation in which you met or a topic you discussed, refer to that. "I remember meeting you at the conference, and we talked about job opportunities in Denver. Tell me your name again!" Or, "As I remember, we talked about the seminar you'd just attended. I'm Todd Watson." That way, you acknowledge that your prior meeting was memorable. Since you've offered your name, your partner will usually follow your cue and give his name.

▶Ask a friend to remind you of the forgotten name. "Jerry, I know I've met that guy over there with the red tie. Remind me of his name."

▶Don't worry about it. Hope that the person's name will occur to you as the conversation goes along. Often, as you begin talking, you'll remember the name.

Give Yourself a Tagline

Often, we give Taglines about ourselves almost automatically. They are short "identifiers" that usually answer your partner's unspoken questions:

▶ "Why are you here?"

▶ "Who are you?"

▶ "How do you relate to me?"

Here are some examples.

Geography Tagline. "Hi, I'm Lois. I'm in the office across from the elevator." Use "geography" to make a connection. I'm here because I work across the hall.

History Tagline. "Hi, I'm Sue, Sue . . . Gost. We played on the company volleyball team together last summer. You've got a great serve." Use your history together to make a connection. You know each other through the volleyball team. You're also throwing in an acknowledgment of your teammate's expertise.

Relationship Tagline. "Hi, I'm Melinda, Melinda . . . Sommers, Harry's secretary." Clarify your relationship to indicate the connection.

Title/Role Tagline. "Hi, I'm George, George . . . Pope. I'm the editor of the company newsletter." Explain what your job is to create a connection.

Reason-for-Attending Tagline. "Hi, I'm Lou, Lou . . . Logan. I'm new in town and interested in meeting people in healthcare." Use your reason for coming to the event to make a connection. That will signal to people that they can help you by introducing you to people in healthcare.

Refer-Me-Please Tagline. You also can create a tagline that allows you to be passed along quickly to a networking partner who is more appropriate for your purposes. You can say, "I'm John Jones. I'm hoping to talk to some people who have used web conferencing and find out which vendors they like best. Do you know anyone who has done a webinar recently?" Chances are, if your first partner doesn't meet your need, she'll pass you along to someone more qualified. This is a shortcut that will help you find what—or who—you are looking for.

Use your Tagline to connect with your conversation partner by telling:

▶ Your location. "I have an office across from the graphics department."

▶ Your history. "Didn't we volunteer together last year at the homeless shelter?"

▶ Your relationship. "I work for the CEO."

▶ Your place in the organization. "I'm in the marketing department."

▶ Your purpose. "I'm hoping to meet people who have experience with ethics training."

▶ How you happened to be in the room. "I'm so glad I got to this meeting. I've admired the speaker from afar for years."

▶ Who you'd like to be passed along to "I'm looking for someone who's savvy about marketing on the Internet."

Yes, Mind Your Manners

Life is more casual today and few people can quote chapter and verse on the protocol of introductions. But it will make you feel more confident to know the rules, so here they are.

Shaking Hands and Standing Up. Anyone who is introduced to anyone else should offer to shake hands. Gender and age used to govern who made the first move. Those distinctions are obsolete today. Reaching out to shake hands should be almost simultaneous. It's proper to stand when introductions are being made unless you are seated in a restaurant or are in some other environment that makes standing difficult.

To Introduce Peers to Each Other. Say either name first. It doesn't matter which one comes first. Use both first and last names and speak distinctly. "Jackie Arnold, this is Rob Baker." Give each some additional information about the other person, if you know them well enough. "Jackie, Rob is on the audit staff. Rob, Jackie is in human resources." Using their names several times will be helpful to them.

To Introduce a Superior to a Subordinate. In today's workplace, we're moving away from focusing on these matters of rank. Nevertheless, to follow the rules, follow this pattern. Say the name of the superior first. "Mr. Brown (or Don, if you use the person's first name), I'd like you to meet Bob Davis. Bob, this is Don Brown." Again, it's helpful to all concerned if you can give some additional information—often just a title will do. "Don, Bob is in our legal department. Bob, Don has been division manager for as long as I've been with the company."

To Introduce a Customer. When introducing customers to people in your business, treat the customer as the superior. Say the customer or client's name first to honor that relationship. "Mr. Smith, I'd like you to meet Mary Jones. Mary, this is Al Smith. We installed one of our systems in his business last week. Al, Mary heads our training staff."

To Introduce Women. It used to be proper always to introduce a man to a woman – that means, you'd treat the woman as if she were the superior, saying her name first. That rule is obsolete and rank should prevail. Since so many people are confused about the rules, don't make any assumptions about the rank of a woman whose name is said first.

To Introduce Older People. It also used to be proper to introduce a younger person to an older person, saying the name of the older person first. Again, today's protocol would be to ignore age.

To Introduce a Person With No Business Status. When introducing someone who has no business status (such as your mother), say the name of the company person first if he or she outranks you. If the company person is a peer or of lower rank, say your mother's name first to honor her.

The Introduction Rule: FIRST IS FOREMOST

The only rule you need to know about introductions: Say the name of the higher-ranking person or the person you want to honor first. First is foremost is the rule. That's all you need to remember.

CHAPTER 9

"What Do You Do?"

In New Zealand, they might ask it this way: "Wot do ye do fer a crust, mate?" In the U.S., it's the inevitable question, the second big question that always comes up in every networking encounter: "What do you do?"

How you answer this oft-asked question is crucial. It's the second "Million-Dollar Moment." But, as was the case with "Who are you?" all too often, the ritual answers we have learned so well, and use so effortlessly, get in the way of building relationships and finding out more about each other.

Why Most Answers Bomb

When people ask, "What do you do?" do you respond with:

▶Your occupation, job type, or category? "I'm an attorney." That's CEMENT. The response falls like a dead weight—a block of cement—at the other person's feet. There may be thirty-seven other attorneys in the room. You just missed the chance to make yourself unique. Your conversation partner is likely to simply say: "Oh . . . nice." Unfortunately, that's the type of comment listeners will probably always make when you describe yourself in this way.

▶Your title? "I'm Assistant Information Systems Manager with the Northeast Division of Management Information Systems, a division of Integrated Information Management, Inc." That's FOG. Giving a title—especially a long, complicated, jargon-filled one—leaves you surrounded by a thick cloud of words. And your conversation partner is likely to say, "Oh . . . nice."

►Your industry? "I'm in real estate." That's THE BLOB. That response puts you right into the middle of the great gray blob of the other twenty-three people your conversation partner knows who are also in real estate. You've missed your chance to tell about your special talents in the real estate industry that make you different from all the other twenty-three. And again, your conversation partner, not knowing what else to say, will probably reply with a polite "Oh . . . nice."

►The name of the organization you work for? "I'm with Disney." That's THE FLAG. That response wraps you in the flag of the organization. You aren't going to be known for your talents and capabilities if you say that; your only identity will be as one of those "Disney people"—a dangerous situation if you ever are laid off.

What's the problem? These commonplace responses to "What do you do?" aren't conversation-builders; they're conversation-stoppers.

Your contact may have learned to deal with CEMENT and THE BLOB by asking questions: "What kind of law do you practice?" "Which one of the real estate companies are you with?" But you won't have made it easy for him to talk with you. And you will have missed the boat when it comes to teaching him anything about your capabilities and talents.

Make the Right Things Happen

Your conversation partner has a TV screen in her head. Most people do. When you tell her about your work, there are two possibilities.

On the one hand, she may see nothing but static—a blizzard on the screen. That's what people see when you have responded to "What do you do?" with CEMENT, FOG, or THE BLOB—nothing. Giving the name of your organization, especially if it's well-known, as in THE FLAG, may feel good for the moment. And your conversation partner will picture your company. But you could get so much more mileage out of your answer. Ask yourself, "What do I want my contact to see on the TV screen in her head? What one thing do I want her to know about me?" When you come up with *that*, you'll know what to say.

Give It Your BEST

Use our formula—the BEST/TEST—to construct your answer. The first sentence of your reply tells the one thing of all your many talents and skills you do BEST. The second sentence gives a brief example and is a TESTimonial to your talents. It should briefly show how you saved the day, served the client, or solved the problem.

Use only ten or fifteen words in your first sentence to tell what you do BEST. Keep it snappy and jargon-free. Aim to be understood by a ten-year-old. Include exciting, colorful, vivid language.

Andy says, "I tried the two ways of answering 'What do you do?' at a recent conference when I wanted to get into conversation with the executive director of the President's Council on Physical Fitness and Sports. When I said, 'I'm with the Association of Pedestrian and Bicycle Professions,' I got a blank stare. I've figured out that, when people hear the association's name, they often think I either run the Tour de France or own a messenger service! But later that day I had a second chance. I tried again, saying, 'I work for an association that helps people find information and resources on how to build more walking and bicycling into their lives and their communities. We just gave a grant that created 300 more miles of trails in Colorado.' The look of interest on the executive director's face was all I needed to convince me that using the BEST/TEST formula to answer 'What do you do?" is much better."

Consider this example. Kathy used to say, "I'm a senior manager with the construction advisory practice of a professional services firm." That answer created a FOG in the listener's mind. But using the BEST/TEST formula Kathy now gets conversations going with this answer: "I help clients when their dream construction project turns into their worst nightmare—you know, when construction projects aren't delivered on time, on budget or to the right quality standards. I just mediated a conflict over construction of a power plant in Asia." Her new answer makes pictures appear on the TV screen in the listener's mind.

Terri used to describe herself as "a marketing consultant," a CEMENT answer. Now, she tells what she does best: "I help people get the word out about their products and services." She updates her

TEST constantly to provide a vivid picture of her succeeding with clients: "Last week, I wrote a news release that got one of my clients, a CPA, on the front page of Tuesday's business section. He's had seven calls so far from prospective clients since the article appeared!" What do you know about Terri from this short anecdote?

She writes news releases that get results for clients. A CPA is her client. Using the BEST/TEST allows Terri to teach you about her Character and her Competence to build the trust that is necessary to establish an effective networking relationship.

Now, imagine that you run into a CPA who says to you, "I want to let women entrepreneurs know about my services for small businesses." Wouldn't Terri's name and expertise pop up in your mental Rolodex™? Assuming you've learned enough about her Character and Competence, wouldn't you mention Terri to this CPA?

By the way, we hope you won't call your answer to the "What do you do?" question an "Elevator Speech" or a "30-second commercial." Those labels devalue and diminish the very important trustbuilding and teaching process that goes on in this ritual. Your answer is not a "commercial." It is a carefully crafted couple of sentences that you will use to spark a conversation and begin to teach your contact about your Character and Competence.

Be Interesting

Rather than eliciting the comment, "Oh . . . nice," when you tell what you do, aim for this comment: "Tell me more." When people asked Buford, "What do you do?" he used to give his title. It was so long that he had to stop and take a breath in the middle: "I'm director of student financial aid in the student affairs division at the University of Missouri (gasp!) Kansas City." And people said, "Oh . . . nice."

Then he came up with another way—a much more interesting way—to put it. He started saying, "I give away $32 million a year. One student we gave a four-year scholarship to just graduated with honors and came by the office to thank us." Did people want to hear more? You bet!

Lisa who's a program analyst at the Department of State, told us in a workshop that she wished she'd known the BEST/TEST formula when she was at a luncheon attended by then Secretary of State Colin Powell. "Powell sat down beside me, introduced himself and asked, 'What do you do?' All I could come up with was, "I work for Mr. Baker." That was such a poor conversation starter that Powell then turned to talk to someone else. I can't blame him! Here's the answer I wish I'd given: 'I design office spaces here at State. We just finished a rush job, doing 880 offices for six different bureaus.'"

Look at Figure 9-1 for some more examples of vivid ways people tell what they do.

FIGURE 9-1. Transforming Your Answer.

Instead Of	Say
"I'm a dietitian." (CEMENT)	"I help people read between the lines on the soup can labels." (BEST)
	"I just testified at a Congressional Committee hearing about the high amount of salt in our foods." (TEST)
"I'm an engineer." (CEMENT)	"I was on the engineering team that figured out how to build a theater nine feet away from the New York subway system." (BEST)
	"We did it without interfering with any of the rehearsals and performances going on directly above us in Carnegie Hall." (TEST)
"I'm the human resources organizational development consultant for the Office of Human Resources Management at the Department of Health and Human Services, regional division office." (FOG)	"I help people learn to fight fair at work." (BEST)
	"This morning, I sat down with two warring teams and convinced them to smoke the peace pipe." (TEST)
"I'm a senior survey methodologist and survey manager with the government consulting firm." (FOG)	"I design surveys for government clients." (BEST)
	"I just wrote one to send to veterans returning from the Iraqi war and I bet on a hunch that we'd get a better response rate if we had an on-line way to answer. Sure enough, responses went up by 20%" (TEST)

(continues)

FIGURE 9-1. Continued.

Instead Of	Say
"I work at Marquette University." (THE FLAG)	"I'm a food critic, party planner and transportation expert." (BEST)
	"I just planned every detail of a meeting in Washington for forty people on our Alumni Board of Directors here at Marquette." (TEST)
"I'm in the travel business." (THE BLOB)	"I send people on vacation." (BEST)
	"I just got a note from one of my clients thanking me for the most stress-free vacation he's ever had." (TEST)

Try These Tips

Say the right *thing in your BEST/TEST.* Don't choose being interesting over teaching people what you *really* want them to know about you. A pharmaceutical saleswoman got people's attention when she said, "I sell drugs." But after thinking it over, she decided that was not what she wanted to teach people. She now says, "I educate doctors about new drugs, so they can give their patients the most up-to-date information on prescriptions."

Tell your talent, not your title. Titles tell what you are, not what you do. Instead, paint a picture in the other person's mind of you in action, you at your best.

Avoid acronyms and jargon. When the person you're talking with is unfamiliar with your "insider lingo" they will feel put off.

Resist the ego trip. If you work for a well-known or prestigious group, resist the urge to bask in that organization's glory. If you must say "I'm with Hallmark," or "I'm at the Department of State," be sure to also include a talent or an example. We guarantee that the name of your organization alone won't start the conversation you want. And worse yet, you just missed the chance to teach someone about your talents and successes.

Ask a question. A variation on the BEST/TEST is to answer "What do you do?" with a question. David asks, "Has your bank ever put your money in somebody else's account?" Whether the answer is yes or no, he says, "I'm working with Federal Reserve banks nationwide to design a system so that never happens again."

Read These Frequently Asked Questions

Here are some questions people ask about the BEST/TEST method.

Q: "Is it *ever* okay to tell my title and the name of the company I work for?"

A: Sure. You can say those things later in the conversation if you wish. But beware. It's a dangerous thing to fall in love with your title and your company. The pleasure you take in introducing yourself with your title and your company affiliation is an indication of your dependency on them for your self-image. In today's volatile economy, you could find yourself out of work tomorrow. (Find more resources at our website, www.FireProofYourCareer.com.)

It's far better to teach people about your abilities. For instance, you might want them to know that you are an outstanding trainer who knows how to convey complicated technical information. Your talents and your reputation will get you your next job, not your current title and company.

Q: "What if I wear several hats?"

A: Prepare several different BEST/TESTs. Select the right one to use depending on whom you are talking to and what you want him to know about you. For instance, when one of your co-authors is talking to meeting planners, she might say, "I get people talking at conventions." (BEST) "I just gave the kickoff keynote on convention networking at the Healthcare Educators annual meeting." (TEST)

When one of us is talking to people in professional services, she might say, "I help lawyers get the most out of their professional memberships and turn contacts into clients." (BEST) "I just finished a four-part seminar for attorneys at McCann, Henry, & Wisecoff." (TEST)

When one of us is talking to people in the publishing industry, she might say, "I wrote the book on networking." (BEST) "A book club just bought 59,400 copies." (TEST)

Q: "Isn't this bragging?"

A: Some people in our workshops say, "Oh, I could never say something like that. I'd feel like I was bragging." But are you? See the "What do you do?" question as an invitation to tell what you're excited about, working on, or proud of. A lot of it has to do with your delivery—so show you were as excited and thrilled as your client. Your body language and tone of voice can show you're excited about the results you bring for your internal or external clients, or the students you serve, or the association members you keep informed.

As the great American humorist Will Rogers once said, "If you done it, it ain't braggin'." If you're talking about your Mercedes Benz, your yacht and your house in Switzerland, that's bragging. But if you're talking about a project you poured your time, talent, and creativity into, that's not bragging.

Another way to make your answer more conversational is to start with a question. Judy does that sometimes. She says, "You know the U.S. government buys millions of dollars of products and services each year? Well, my clients come to me for advice on whether or not selling to the government is a good bet for them. I was so pleased yesterday when one client called and said, 'I think your advice just saved us about $200,000 and a lot of headaches.'"

When you're asked what you do, the best way to start a conversation is to be enthusiastic and specific about your accomplishments. How else will people learn what to count on you for, what you're good at, whom they should refer to you, and what opportunities they should send your way?

Q: "How will I know when I have a good answer to the question, 'What do you do?'"

A: Ask yourself these three questions:

1. Does my answer give a specific, positive picture of me succeeding, me doing what I want to be known for? Does it teach about my Character, my Competence? Does it show what I want to do more of?

2. Does my answer encourage people to say, "Tell me more?" Does it invite questions and conversation with-

out being maddeningly mysterious? The real estate agent who merely says "I'm a miracle worker" is being too cagey. She needs to add ". . . for home buyers." Her TEST can further clarify her claim as she says, "I just found a house for a newly married couple who both use wheelchairs—and at a price they can afford in a neighborhood they love."

3. Do I deliver my answer in an excited, upbeat way, in a tone of voice that expresses my delight in serving my customers or solving the problems, rather than sounding full of myself?

Q: "What should I do if the person I'm talking with gives me CEMENT (her job type), FOG (her title), or THE BLOB (her industry)?"

A: Ask questions designed to draw out specific examples, learn about special expertise, or hear about unique projects. Ask:

▶ "What's a typical day like in your work?"

▶ "Tell me about a recent project you've been working on."

▶ "What have you been doing this week."

▶ "What's your favorite project these days at work?"

Q: "I'm in a technical field. I have a Ph.D. I can't imagine being so folksy—especially when I'm with my peers and everyone is trying to one-up the other person."

A: It's okay to use your title or the jargon of your profession if you are speaking to other people in the same specialty. But be sure to supplement that with a vivid TESTimonial, so that people have a clear idea of your expertise.

Q: "I hate what I do. I'm just an office manager. It's so boring. I'm trying to change careers. What should I say?"

A: If you don't like what you are doing, don't talk about it. Instead talk about the five percent of your job you do like or what you have done in the past or what you want to do in the future. Mary, who posed the question, now describes the part of her job she likes the most: "I'm an expert scheduler and organizer." (BEST) "Last year, when my company relocated, I managed the move. It was so exciting to see us go from an up-and-running office into thousands of boxes and back out again in record time and with a minimum of trauma." (TEST)

Give contacts specifi examples of projects so that they can describe to others—accurately and vividly—what you do.

Q: "Won't I need several answers depending on who I'm talking to and how well they know my kind of work?"

A: Absolutely! We recommend you have four or five answers you're comfortable giving. One might be for an informal setting like a backyard barbecue or when you're at the swimming pool with your kids. One might be for use internally and designed to teach people in your organization how your work contributes to the bottom line. Another might be for when you're at a conference, designed to teach how your skills would apply in a new career arena you're thinking of moving to.

Q: "How can I keep my answers to 'What do you do?' from sounding stilted or canned? People aren't used to hearing something this long or detailed."

A: True. A BEST/TEST answer will set you apart from the crowd. Say your answer with enthusiasm and as if you know the listener will be interested. Practice it until you know it as well as you know your own name. Be sure to keep your TEST short. Your answer is not an item on your resumé and shouldn't sound like "resumé-speak." Keep the language conversational and jargon-free so it flows off your tongue easily. Watch for people's reactions and modify your answers until you get the responses you want.

CHAPTER 10

"What Are We Going to Talk About?"

There's one conversation that everybody knows, word-for-word. You can hear it at networking events all across the U.S., from Tacoma, Washington, to Tampa, Florida. It goes like this:

"Hi, how are you?"
"Good. How are you?"
"Not bad. What's new?"
"Not much. What's new with you?"
"Not much. Been real busy."
"Me too. Good to see you."
"You too. We'll have to get together sometime."
"Great idea. I'll give you a call."
"Well, bye. See you later."

This is a conversation in search of a topic! Without one or more topics that *you* want to talk about, you'll waste your time in purposeless chit-chat like that one-size-fits-all conversation.

It pays to be prepared to talk about topics you care about. Having an Agenda—a plan for your networking conversations—is vital.

Listen for Your Cue

Two cues should prompt you to say to yourself, "Time to use my Agenda."

One cue is hearing, "How are you?" or "What's new?"

The other cue is the pause, as you and your conversation partner search for something to talk about. Often that pause comes just after you've finished talking about what you both do—and just before the conversation about the weather or the ball scores!

Do you wonder, "How can I direct the conversation to my business or to topics that are really important to me?" Here's how to manage the third "Million-Dollar Moment."

Use Success Stories to Tell What's New

When somebody asks her, "What's new?" Ilsa says, "I'm training for a marathon. If I tell people that, then they'll ask me, the next time we meet, 'How's the marathon training going?' That keeps me motivated, and committed to my goal." Another reason for talking about the marathon is that she is looking for pledges for the charity run.

When somebody asks him, "What's new?" Sam says, "I've moved my business. My new location is right next to the Metro—and the rent is actually lower!" The reason he gives for choosing that topic is that he wants to show how easy it is to get to his graphic design business.

Both Ilsa and Sam have good answers and good reasons for their answers to "What's new?"

But all too often, people reply, "Not much. What's new with you?" and sink into another one of those superficial conversations like the one at the beginning of this chapter.

> When someone asks "What's new?" tell a Success Story that shows you saving the day, solving the problem, or serving the customer.

The best reply to "What's new?" is to tell a Success Story. A Success Story is a short, punchy anecdote. It teaches your conversation partner what you do, what you're interested in (like Ilsa), how you serve customers or clients, something important about your business (like Sam) or what you or your firm have to offer. For more information on constructing your Success Stories, see Chapter 11.

Figure Out Your Agenda

More than 85 percent of people we surveyed as they arrived at networking events hadn't figured out exactly why they'd come. They knew they wanted something, but hadn't figured out what! They hadn't thought about who they wanted to meet, what they wanted to find out, and how they were going to achieve their goals. They didn't know what they wanted to share, tell people about, pass along. Predictably, about the same percentage of people, surveyed on their way out, said they wished they'd gotten more out of the event.

To be an effective networker, have a clear purpose in mind before you begin talking with people. That purpose comes from knowing what's on your ever-changing Agenda. As you focus on your Agenda, you'll feel eager and excited about connecting with people.

> **Make an Agenda of things to talk about, and don't leave home without it.**

Your networking Agenda is a mental or written list of what you have To Give and what you want To Get.

Since we each have unique purposes, we each have unique Agendas.

Bill, a teacher, has a small real estate business on the side. He was elated when he finally found an accountant he trusted and enjoyed working with. In the weeks that followed, he enthusiastically recommended her when talking with other business owners. At the same time, Bill was looking for someone to work for him part-time, doing mailings and keeping his database up to date. He had something to *give* in his conversations—his recommendation of an accountant; he had something he was trying to *get* in his conversations—the name of a qualified person who might like to work part time. He had an Agenda.

Using this chapter, you'll learn how to construct your personal Agenda to focus on the things you want To Get and, equally important, the things you have To Give as you make connections with other people. Having an Agenda will energize and empower you so that you'll benefit from your networking. And using your Agenda will help you uncover the commonalities and needs that move the relationship from the Associates to the Actors Stage. You'll feel comfortable and capable of enjoying yourself, making contact, gathering information, and seeking out opportunities.

You may have dreaded networking situations in the past because you felt you didn't have anything to talk about. Actually, when it comes to topics, the problem is *not* that there's *nothing* to talk about. The problem is that there's *too much* to talk about! Hundreds of topics a day come crashing in on you via newspaper, TV, radio, e-mail, junk mail, and the Internet. Often no one topic looks that much more interesting than any other. So it's hard, perhaps impossible, to select from all of the ideas racing around in your head. An Agenda simplifies the situation. And you automatically care about—and have energy for—the topics on your own Agenda list.

Begin with the Right Side

There are two sides to your Agenda: what you want To Get and what you have To Give. Most people, as they think about networking, focus on what's in it for them. That's not the right place to begin. In fact, the second biggest mistake people make about networking (after not being strategic) is to think that it's about getting. It's not about getting. It's about giving.

Russell Simmons, cofounder of Def Jam Records, says the following in Business 2.0, an online magazine: "You get a lot of benefit from giving, not from taking. You have to fill a void, give people something that's meaningful and useful."

Giving—not taking—is the way to build your network. It's not just a nice thing to do. It's the smart thing to do.

> There are two sides networking: giving and getting. You are only in control of on side—guess which one. It only makes sense to work on th side you control 100 percent.

Psychologists have discovered a quirk of human nature that we call The Reciprocity Principle. It goes like this: If you give somebody something, he will try to give you something back. It gets even better. If you give somebody something, he will insist on giving you *more* than you gave him.

Doesn't that sound exactly like what you want to happen when you're networking? So, to plug into The Reciprocity Principle, give first, give freely.

You're actually in control of only half of the networking process—the giving part. Does it make sense to focus on the getting part—something you have little control over?

Have lots to give and give generously. Be helpful to others. Often, you'll benefit from contact with someone whom you can't immediately—or perhaps ever—pay back. Believe in the great network in the sky—that if you give, you will get—somehow, somewhere, someday.

> **The Reciprocity Principle: When you give people something, they will insist on giving you even more back.**

Five years ago, an executive gave Ellen some career advice. This year, when she received the Member of the Year award from her professional association, she mentioned the executive in her acceptance speech, thanked him, and told how she felt inspired to mentor others because of his help early in her career.

Giving positions you as a resource. As Donna, a senior sales representative, says, "Think of yourself as networking at a larger scale than giving information about your business. I might help a woman I know find a spot on a non-profit board, for instance, not because I know I'll get business from it, but rather because I want people to see me as the person you come to when you don't know where to find something. I want to be seen as someone who knows a lot of resources and people."

At first, it may seem that you are giving more than you are getting from your networking relationships. If so, you are networking the right way.

What Do You Have to Give?

People often scratch their heads and say, "Give? I don't know what I have to give." To create your To Give list, think about your accomplishments, skills, enthusiasms, and resources.

Most of us really do have plenty to give—ideas, expertise, phone numbers, introductions to other people. The possibilities are endless. But, if you have a hard time figuring out exactly what you can offer, try using this formula.

Think to yourself, "Give MORE."

M = Methods. Can you make life easier for your contacts?

▶ "My expertise on how—and how not—to build a brick patio."

▶ "Information about how to run web conferences as an alternative to on-site training."

▶ "How to negotiate the best deal on severance if you've been laid off."

O = Opportunities. Can you alert people to an opportunity?

▶ "An apartment to sublet for six months."

▶ "Rex kittens (extremely short-haired cats for people with allergies)."

▶ "A job opening at Allied Sciences."

R = Resources. Can you offer someone or something?

▶ "The name and phone number of a great band for weddings and parties."

▶ "The name of my veterinarian who makes house calls."

▶ "A great article I just read on how people react to website design."

▶ "A place—my conference room—to hold meetings."

E = Enthusiasms. Are you excited about something?

▶ "My professional association. Our programs for professional development are terrific!"

▶ "Taking jazz singing lessons from one of the best teachers in Washington, D.C."

As you become more aware of what you have to give to others, you'll always be able to narrow down the universe of topics to a list of things you want to talk about. The things you have to give automatically become topics. These topics connect you with the people you meet. They also let people know what to count on you for. Listen for or create moments to offer what's on your To Give list.

Being prepared to give means taking stock of your accomplishments, resources, skills, and enthusiasms. It means acknowledging that you are a unique and special human being with a contribution to make. If you wish you had more to give others, it may be a sign that you need to stock up. Do more. Experience more. Learn more. Risk more. Take a negotiation skills class. Learn Thai cooking. Take that vacation you've been talking about. Go ahead with

Get ready to give. Before an event, list three resources, tips, or opportunities to tell people about.

the catering business you've dabbled in for so long. Anything you become enthusiastic about becomes something to share. Your enthusiasms are things you're so excited about that you'd talk to anybody, anywhere, anytime about them. When you live to the fullest, you'll just naturally have lots of resources, experiences, and opinions to give to others.

Having things to give makes it easy for you to go from just associating with people to interacting and exchanging with them. When you Listen Generously and find resources and ideas to give, you automatically move from the Associate Stage into the Actor Stage with your contact. As you give, you provide evidence of your Character and Competence. You create trust so that your contacts want to send opportunities your way.

What Do You Want to Get?

After you've thought through what you have to give, it's time to think about getting. The list of things you want to find, connect with, create, understand, learn, and know about also is endless. Look at your desk; look at your life. What problems are you trying to solve? What opportunities do you want to investigate? What are your upcoming challenges?

To help you jog your memory, think, "Get REAL." Notice the examples.

R = *Results.* What outcome do you want?

▶ "Office furniture I can afford."

▶ "Training so I can get up to speed on my computer graphics software."

▶ "Tips on growing BIG tomatoes."

E = *Expertise.* What do you want to know about?

▶ "A good, convenient day camp for my nine-year-old."

▶ "Tips on appearing on a TV talk show."

▶ "The best way to find good employees for my start-up."

A = *Access.* Who or what do you need to find?

▶ "A part-time secretary with a background in the health field."

▶ "A publisher for my book."

▶ "A good caterer for our next sales meeting."

L = *Leads.* Who do you need to meet?

▶ "People who are thinking of selling their homes and moving to retirement complexes."

▶ "A veterinarian to join my business referral group."

▶ "Someone who knows about careers in training and development."

▶ "An experienced emcee for the Chamber of Commerce Trade Show."

Give and Get with Ease

In our workshops, we ask people to make lists of things they'd like To Give and To Get. When they realize they do have a lot to offer, they immediately feel more comfortable about making conversation with purpose and pizzazz. When they bring what they really need to the surface of their minds, they immediately feel more eager to network. We ask people to choose one item from each list—one thing they have To Give and one thing they'd like To Get—and write both items on stick-on nametags.

The people in the room become a living bulletin board, a human swap meet. They talk with each other about what they've written on their nametags. As they begin to discover each other, the energy level in the room heats up, the excitement builds, and the noise level rises. Figure 10-1 shows some of the things a group of our workshop participants wanted To Give and To Get.

You'll notice that in this Sample Agenda there are no exact matches between the have To Give and want To Get items. If you don't know of a classy restaurant in New York City, introduce your conversation partner to Phil, who used to live there. With an Agenda, you'll be able to find common interests with your conversation partners. What counts is that on any of these topics, the talk will be meaningful and useful—and therefore valuable—for someone. As in the rest of life, sometimes you'll give and sometimes

FIGURE 10-1. Sample Agenda Items.

To Give	To Get
Information on owning your own business.	Someone to buy my Boston condo.
How to start a job strategy and support group.	The best antique mall in Nashville.
Recipes for big crowds.	Tips on using my new BlackBerry.™
Good restaurants in Toronto.	Speakers for our state conference.
Fund raising ideas for non-profits.	Help with an association chapter history project.
What it's like to be a corporate trainer.	An apartment for my mother to sublet.
My car! It's for sale!	Tips on buying a house at the Lake of the Ozarks.
Where to ski out West.	A place in New York City to take clients out to dinner next week.

you'll get. Clarify your Agenda and talk with people about the topics on it. Author and seminar leader Zig Ziglar says, "You can have everything in life you want—if you help enough other people get what they want."

When you go public with your Agenda like this, networking becomes an exciting process of search and connection.

Now, you probably aren't going to actually write an item from your Agenda on your nametag the next time you go to a business or social event. But, you can prepare for any occasion by making a written list of items you have To Give and want To Get. Put the list in your pocket. You won't need to refer to it; you'll simply feel the confidence that comes from being prepared.

You can assume that the other people in the room—even if they don't realize it—also have Agendas. Discovering their Agendas—and following your own Agenda—will become a whole new approach to networking. "Chance," it is said, "favors the prepared mind." Preparing your Agenda is preparing your mind for making great connections.

Stan is vice president of sales for a burglar alarm company. He has twenty-four salespeople spread over a four-state area. Figure 10-2 is an Agenda he used at a networking event.

Did Stan find what he was looking for? At the end of the meeting, he had the names of two chiropractors, three businesses that agreed to donate items for the auction, and a Boston contact.

When someone asked him, "What's new?" Stan started talking about the Cajun cooking class he was taking. His conversation partner told Stan about a store that sells nothing but spices that he's going to investigate.

With an Agenda, you'll see results from your networking every time.

Practice Agenda-Making

Think of an upcoming networking situation. Take a moment and list some things you'd like To Give in your conversations with others—resources, ideas, skills, experiences, talents, and enthusiasms, for example. Then list what you'd like To Get, find, connect with, know more about, and create in your life. Be as specific as possible. If you put "Happiness" on your want To Get list, for example, you'll be disappointed because no one can give that to you.

FIGURE 10-2. Stan's Agenda.

To Give	To Get
Information on the new video-based sales training package I use.	Magazine articles or books for my sales people on how to start referral groups.
Ideas on how to do a trade show booth that gets attention.	Job leads for my brother-in-law.
The name of an excellent chiropractor.	Businesses that will donate items for the hospital auction.
How to cook Cajun.	Contacts who can recommend people I might hire in Boston.

Go Public with Your Agenda

The cardinal rule about anyone's networking Agenda is this: "If there's no mystery, there's no manipulation." Managing conversations is quite different from manipulating other people. Managing is okay; manipulating is not. Effective networking is based on saying what you want and making sure that you take every opportunity to contribute to the success of others by giving anything you can.

Were you brought up to believe that saying outright what you want is pushy, self-centered, and overbearing? Were you taught that you should not see people as opportunities? Many people were. Sometimes, as a kid, you might have had to toss out subtle clues or be indirect to get what you wanted. As an adult, it's

> In networking, be up front, be honest. If there's no mystery, there's no manipulation.

best to be direct. Tell your contacts, straight out, what's on your Agenda. Your honesty about your purposes will increase your sense of competence and professionalism. With these new ground rules for networking, the people you meet become opportunities for you, and you become an opportunity for them.

Here's a surefire test to determine if your Agenda is manipulative. Ask yourself, "How would I feel if my Agenda were the headline on the front page of tomorrow morning's newspaper: *Joe Jackson Hunts Job in Healthcare?* What if everybody knew what I wanted? What if they could see right through the subtle clues to what I actually have in mind? Would they feel good about me and my purpose? Would I?" If the answer is yes, your Agenda item is a good one to talk about.

Avoid asking for information that people normally are paid to provide. Don't describe a legal problem you're having and ask for advice from a lawyer at a networking event. Don't describe a problem you're having with your computer and ask for advice from a computer consultant you meet at a party. On the other hand, it makes sense to find out what kinds of cases a lawyer handles. That kind of information would be acceptable and might be valuable in the future, both to you and to the lawyer, whose name and specialty would then be on file in your mental Rolodex.™

Be prepared to be spontaneous.

Get comfortable telling people how they might be helpful to you in the future. Imagine that you're in a networking situation and complete the following sentence: "I'd like to know you better because . . ."

You could say, "I'd like to know you better because I'd like to know more about what you do as a marketing manager," or "I'd like to stay in touch so we can share strategies about how to make our home-based businesses grow."

How would you feel about going public with the reason? Perhaps you'd like to know this person better because he could be in a position to hire you some day. Is there any benefit in keeping that Agenda hidden? What could be the benefits of sharing that reason with the person? Perhaps you'd like to know this person better because she could probably refer potential clients to you. Is there any reason you can think of that you shouldn't tell her that?

Sally, who owns a tutoring business that employs forty-two tutors, said to the principal of a private school, "I'd like to become known to you because I imagine people often ask you to recommend tutors for their kids."

Corrine, who has her own training company, had lunch with Diana, who is in the marketing department of a greeting card company. Corrine was aboveboard about her Agenda and said to Diana,

"I hope that, when you need training, you'll think of me. I'd love to work with you on a project." A few days later, Corrine saw a column by Humorist Dave Barry making fun of an ad he'd seen for a service that would send cards to your friends and family for you after you were dead. She knew Diana would get a kick out of it, so she sent her a copy of the column. It's little things that build relationships.

Exchange Something

If you still have negative feelings about accepting help from others or being beholden to others, focus your energy on making an exchange. The way to make a fair exchange is to offer something equally valuable. Give something back in the conversation.

One thing you *can* give at any time is appreciation. Take the time to say "Thank you" to people who help you. Make your thanks prompt. Write a note that same day. In the note, be specific about what Jack did for you: "Thank you for giving me Omar's phone number." Tell Jack what you did with the information. That lets Jack know you thought it was important. "I have called Omar and set up an appointment for next Tuesday." Being specific does something else. It could be that Jack will see Omar between now and next Tuesday. Your note may help Jack to remember to mention you. Now, that's networking!

If you are uncomfortable with the idea of going after what you want, remind yourself that people are free to choose. You will certainly say "No" when someone asks for information or offers a service or product you don't want. Trust your conversation partner to say "No" if you offer something he doesn't want or ask for something he isn't comfortable giving.

If you are uncomfortable with the idea of "selling yourself," think of it as giving others the opportunity to take advantage of (in a positive way) your expertise, your talent, your training. You're a resource to them. Believe in yourself and promote yourself. If you offer a service or resource that no one wants right then, what have you lost? Nothing. What have you gained? Others may tuck that information away and use it later.

Build every relationship for the long term. Never assume that you can use and discard people. Harriet remembers: "I ran into a woman at the swimming pool. We'd taught first grade together years ago. We hadn't kept in touch, but we hadn't burned any bridges either. When I was looking for new clients, I remembered seeing her at the pool. She'd told me that her husband was a new manager and felt like he was in over his head. I sent her a brochure about my consulting services. A few weeks later, her husband called me for coaching on management skills."

The idea of the Agenda is a powerful one. It will help your networking be more pleasurable, purposeful, and profitable. Share it. Teach others about the idea of the Agenda, and you will increase your chances of getting what you want, but not at anyone else's expense.

A light bulb went on for one of our workshop participants. She said, "Oh, I get it. You've got to be prepared to be spontaneous!"

CHAPTER 11

Make Conversation Flow

When we ask people to describe what happens in a good conversation, here's what they say:

"There's lots of give and take."

"We move from one topic to the next easily."

"I feel comfortable and listened to."

"I learn a lot about the other person."

"I get a good picture of what she's like and what she's interested in."

"We find out what we have in common."

"Time seems to pass quickly."

"It's easy to shut out the distraction of lots of other conversations going on nearby."

"We talk a long time without running out of things to say."

"Things just flow."

So what do people do to make conversations flow so easily? They rely on three conversational skills to enjoy, explore, and exchange when they're talking with people. Good conversations happen when you Listen Generously, are Seriously Curious, and tell Success Stories from your own experience. Some of these ideas will help you begin a conversation with someone new; others can be used as you Follow Through with contacts you've known for some time. Put these tools to use in your next conversation.

Listen Generously

Networking doesn't mean doing all the talking. The first thing good conversationalists do is give others a chance to talk. Listening Generously means hearing not only the words, but also the *needs* of your conversation partner. As you explore a variety of topics, be alert for opportunities to offer a resource, an idea, an introduction, or just a word of encouragement.

Listening is *not* just waiting for your turn to talk. Unfortunately, many people act that way in conversations—impatiently waiting *instead* of listening. Listening is work. Don't think of it as a passive activity where you just nod every once in a while as you wait for your turn. Listening is active. To be a good listener, give your undivided attention and focus. You *speak* at a rate of about 150 words a minute; but you can *think* more than 500 words a minute. That's one reason you must train yourself to pay attention rather than allow your mind to wander off on tangents. Listening is a challenge. Networking venues are often noisy. You'll probably be trying to listen in a room where lots of other lively conversations are going on. People retain only a small fraction of what they hear. But if you use the tactics in this chapter, you should be able to do much better at the quiet side of networking.

Use Your EARS

Let the EARS formula remind you to listen better.

E = Encourage your partner. Nod, indicate with your body language that you are following what he's saying.

A = Acknowledge your partner. Restate or sum up her point of view.

R = Respond to your partner. Comment, ask questions to get more information, provide information or answers.

S = Save what's being said. Mentally store important pieces of information for future reference.

How Listening Generously Pays Off

You'll reap these five benefits as you listen attentively:

1. *You'll stand out.* Giving true attention is so rare (especially at networking events, where people have a tendency to glance

around the room to see who else is there) that you will make a positive impression. Ken says, "I create an imaginary bubble around me and the person I'm talking with. Six elephants could dance through the room, and I probably wouldn't notice." You can bet people remember talking with him.

2. *You'll find out how to Follow Through.* Listen for what's on the other person's Agenda. Listen for his challenges, interests, and enthusiasms. Bill heard a need as James talked about moving from a downtown office to a home office. A few days later, Bill sent James an article about home office design. Bill isn't selling file cabinets. He's a computer coach who sees business value in becoming known by giving first.

Listen for your contact's Agenda

Remember, it takes six to eight contacts with someone before you know each other well enough to have established a long-term business relationship. So listen for reasons to stay in touch.

3. *You'll develop a reputation as a great connector.* Who would your conversation partner like to meet? To find out, listen. When Carla introduced herself as an interior designer who focuses on the senior citizen market, Mitzi immediately said, "I want to introduce you to Hank. He's an expert on marketing to the 50-plus generation." Listen for links, what people have in common. "You went to the University of Chicago? So did Dan. Let me take you over and introduce you." Or, "You're on the program committee for your women's network at work? Sherrie's active in her company's network. Would you like to meet her?"

When you become known as somebody who knows everybody, people will call you and ask you if you know someone who. . . . As you link people together, you give to them and plug into The Reciprocity Principle. They will try to give you something back.

4. *You'll be able to bridge to what's on your Agenda.* Suppose you and your conversation partner are talking about the horrors of business travel. You'd like to bridge to your need to find a conference center for your sales meeting. Listen carefully and make the transition. "Sounds like you've clocked a lot of miles to far away places, Fred. You know, that reminds me. I'm looking for something close to home, and you might be able to help. I wonder if you know

of any conference centers within about 75 miles of the city. I need to find a place for my June meeting of 200 salespeople."

5. *You'll learn something.* There's an old saying: "A good listener is not only popular, but after a while, he knows something." As you listen, you'll increase your understanding and knowledge of the topic under discussion.

Carlos, an architect, was visiting friends in San Francisco. At a dinner party they gave, he met Bill, who is in the import/export business. Carlos couldn't imagine what they could possibly have in common, but he listened intently as Bill explained how he sought out the work of artists around the world. Several months later, one of Carlos's clients wanted an unusual work of art for the lobby of his new building. Carlos remembered Bill and enlisted his help in finding just what the client wanted.

Be Seriously Curious

When we were four years old, we were curious about everything. Nothing escaped our interest. Everything got our undivided attention. But somewhere along the way, we have learned to look cool, as if we've seen it all, as if nothing surprises us. To be a great connector, re-connect with some of that four-year-old curiosity. Find a role model. Anyone under the age of five will do. Notice the questions he asks, the energy he has for finding out.

Seeing the fisherman bring his boat up onto the beach, four-year-old Matt ran up to have a look at the catch. He had dozens of questions: "Why is that one striped, but this one is spotted?" "Does that kind grow any bigger?" "Are all of these fish good to eat?" "Which one is poisonous?" "Do you like to touch them?" "Can they make noise under water?"

Asking good questions is the second tool you need to make conversation flow. Questions help you uncover a need or a commonality and move more quickly into the Actors Stage of relationship building, where you are actively exchanging information.

Often people ask questions that are too broad, too vague, and too ritualistic. They ask "What's new," or "Hi, Bob, what's going on?" One of the very best questions—because it narrows the scope—is "What have you been working on lately?"

Learn more about being Seriously Curious from these ten tips:

1. *Organize some openers.* Do your brain a favor and, ahead of time, think of several openers. What could you say to start a conversation with the person sitting next to you at a workshop? How would you begin a conversation with someone at the hors d'oeuvres table? Here are some possibilities:

▶ "The title of this session, 'How To Stop the Brain Drain,' really grabbed my attention. Is your organization finding that a problem, too?"

▶ "Are you a first-timer like me or a long-time member?"

▶ "This speaker made a good point about career security. What do you think of her ideas?"

2. *Ask about origins and history.* Asking about beginnings is a good way to hear about how people got where they are and to learn more about their Character and Competence. Ask:

▶ "How did the project begin?"

▶ "How did you meet your business partner?"

▶ "How did you get into marketing?"

▶ "How did you come up with this unusual packaging idea?"

3. *Notice other people.* When you say, "I noticed you were on the edge of your seat during the speech," it's a compliment. When you take the time to notice people out loud, you'll find that the interaction deepens and the conversation becomes more personal. You've let the other person know that he is visible to you, that you are thinking about him. That's when a relationship begins. Here are some examples.

▶ "You seemed to really enjoy giving that presentation. Have you always felt comfortable talking in front of groups?"

▶ "I noticed your pin. It's very beautiful. Is there a story behind it?" (Often, people ask, "Where did you get it?" Avoid that question. It could sound envious or even predatory—as if you want to go right out and buy one just like it.)

▶ "I noticed you made sure everyone got a chance to give their ideas in the meeting. Does that come naturally or did you learn some techniques from the class the company offers?"

4. *Appreciate other people.* When was the last time someone told you something they appreciated about you, for no reason, out of the blue? Maybe you were a little embarrassed, but wasn't it wonderful? Didn't it brighten your day and give you a special connection to that person? Your willingness to give appreciation to other people is a sign of your confidence and strength. As your capacity for gratitude grows, your ability to give grows. No phony baloney stuff here, please. Just ask yourself from time to time, when you're with people, "What do I appreciate about this person? What would feel good to acknowledge about this person?"

5. *Take clichés seriously.* Listen for clichés and know how to handle them. When someone says, "How are you?" and you reply, "Fine," you've just completed a dead-end routine. Coping with these ritual conversations is one reason people hate to network. The question "How are you?" is too big, too open-ended. Here are some tactics that will help you move from a ritual conversation into one that goes somewhere:

If you're bored, bore in. Take the cliché one step further, explore it. Or make it more personal. Or make your response unexpected and playful.

If you ask, "How have you been?" and your partner replies, "Busy," ask:

▶ "What's a typical busy day like for you?"

▶ "What do you do on a busy weekend?"

▶ "If you decided tomorrow not to be busy any more, what would you quit doing?"

▶ "Do you remember times in your life that you haven't been as busy? Did you like it?"

6. *Do something about the weather.* Everybody talks about the weather, but nobody does anything about it. How can you say something different or personal about it? How can you move the conversation to a more business-like topic? As with other ritual topics, if you are Seriously Curious, the weather can become interesting. If someone says, "Terrible weather we're having," then ask:

▶ "Have you ever lived anyplace where the weather's worse?"

▶ "I find the weather really affects my energy? Do you notice that too?"

If Dan says, "What a beautiful day!" you might ask:

▶ "What are you doing now that it's warm outside?"

▶ "Do ups and downs in the weather affect your sales much?"

Asking serious questions about a superficial topic turns your partner into an ordinary expert. Notice how these questions lead to more important topics. Your partner's answers provide clues to new topics to follow up on.

Don't forget your Agenda. Eleanor says, "My interest in talking about the weather was zero until I started planning for retirement. Now, I direct the weather conversation to my Agenda, saying, 'Yes, this humidity's a killer. It's recently hit me that when I retire, I can live anywhere on earth. Where do you suppose has the best weather?" Even boring weather conversations will come alive when you tie them to your real interests or needs.

7. *Encourage dialogue*. Good conversation is a dialogue, not a monologue. Plan to talk only about 50 percent of the time, and you'll be remembered as someone who was interested as well as interesting. Notice people's body language—it often signals when they have something to add. Check out whether people are with you by saying things like, "Have you ever experienced that?" or "Is this something you're dealing with at work, too?" Look at Figure 11-1 for the difference.

FIGURE 11-1. Going for Dialogue.

A Monologue	A Dialogue
Ask no questions of the other person.	Ask the other person questions.
Talk more than two or three minutes.	Get others involved after a minute or two.
Answer your own questions.	Wait for others to answer.
Fill up the silence.	Pause, be comfortable with a little silence.
Ignore new people who join your group.	Involve new people who join your group.
Keep talking, no matter what.	Notice and respond to reactions.

8. *Dig for gold.* Imagine that someone says to you, "My life is just crazy right now." That's a goldmine statement. If you dig deeper, you might find the mother lode. Surprisingly enough, most people respond with, "Oh, me too." They ignore the obvious question waiting to be asked, "What's going on that's crazy?" In one such exchange, Lee got a surprising answer: "I'm interviewing people for a new job we've created in our department." Lee applied for that job and was hired. Wasn't she glad she decided to go for the gold?

As Jean and Chuck talked before the board meeting started, he said, "What a week! I've never seen anything like it." Instead of responding with the usual cliché, "I know what you mean," Jean went for the goldmine, saying "Tell me more. What's going on in your life?" Chuck said, "We're trying to find a cat sitter to live in our house this summer." Jean suggested her boss's daughter, a college student who loved cats.

9. *Interview people.* Imagine you're writing a magazine article about your conversation partner. Ask profile questions. These are the kinds of questions you may have seen in the American Express ads.

Put a few of your favorites from this list in your repertoire in case a conversation lags. Many of them are somewhat playful and likely to encourage a more personal response than some of the questions that are more conventional. Don't be afraid to try them.

▶ A typical day in your life?

▶ Personal philosophy?

▶ Business philosophy?

▶ Favorite anything: TV show, magazine, singer, song, performer, music, website, author, book, movie, actor, actress, meal, snack?

▶ Favorite gadget?

▶ Favorite thing to do on a Sunday afternoon?

▶ Personal hero?

▶ Motto?

▶ Dream vacation?

▶ What your Dad (Mom) always told you?

▶ Worst job?

▶ Biggest obstacle you had to overcome in your life?

▶ What people in high school thought you were like?

▶ What you wish you could stop doing?

▶ Someone you'd give anything to meet?

▶ Something you hope you never have to do?

▶ What you'd be doing if you weren't doing what you are doing?

▶ One thing you'd like to change about your work or business?

▶ Advice you'd give young people?

▶ What you've learned about life?

▶ Issues that matter to you? Action you take in support of those issues?

Answer the question yourself first if you feel that the question might be seen as intrusive. Obviously this kind of thing can be overdone; you'll want to be sensitive and appropriate. Use a playful tone of voice. It's fun to try profile questions on people you think you know well: your business partner, your teenager, your parents, your office mates, or even your boss.

10. *Invite other people to talk.* Want people to tell you more? Prompt them to continue the conversation. Encourage your conversation partners. If you've been talking about executive coaching for employees, ask, "And, how about your company? Do you coach executives?"

Jim Collins, author of *Built to Last* and *Good to Great*, says: "If you want to have an interesting conversation, be interested. If you want to meet interesting people, be interested in the people you meet—their lives, their history, their story. Where are they from? How did they get there? What have they learned? By practicing the art of being interested, the majority of people become fascinating teachers; nearly everyone has an interesting story to tell."

Tell Success Stories

There's a third skill that will make your conversations flow—storytelling.

At lunch with a client, on the flight to Denver with your boss, with the hiring manager as you wait for your job interview to begin, at the health club—wherever you are, your skill at telling stories will make people enjoy talking with you. Stories help the listener see you in action. Your anecdote puts a vivid picture in Joe's head so he remembers to refer you to his client. Your anecdote teaches Susan what you're good at or what you might be looking for so you can move to the Actor Stage of relationship building. Your example shows

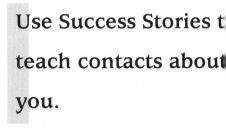

Use Success Stories t

teach contacts about

you.

Mary more about your Character and Competence, so she feels confident recommending you for the promotion. To have memorable conversations, hone your ability to tell stories.

How good are you at telling a brief story, example, or anecdote that teaches people about you—your interests, your challenges, your talent? Don't be put off by the word *success*. Of course, we're not advising you to brag. That would detract from your Character and Competence. But if you construct your Success Story carefully, it can do a lot for you: It can give a vivid example of your expertise, enhance your credibility, teach people to trust you, and make people want to do business with you.

When someone at a networking event asked Carrie, who has her own PR business, "What's new," here's what she said. "I was really scrambling last week. I was in the middle of creating a brochure for Oak Tree Mall, and my office was flooded after that big rainstorm. So, I rented a computer, worked at home, and got the layout to the client on deadline, just as I had promised. Boy, was he happy!"

Here's what our workshop participants said Carrie's story taught them about her:

▶ "She won't let anything make her miss a deadline."

▶ "She's reliable."

▶ "She'll do what it takes to get the job done on time."

▶ "She's resourceful."

▶ "She doesn't give up."

▶ "She handles crises well."

▶ "She's doing work for a prestigious client, so she must be good."

▶ "You can trust her; she'll come through."

As you can see, you can get a lot of mileage out of a good Success Story: a reputation for going to heroic lengths to meet your deadlines, for delighting clients, for having a top business in town as a client. Best of all, it gives your contact a concrete picture of exactly what you do.

Construct Your Story Carefully

Before you go to your next networking event, where you're sure to be asked the inevitable question, "What's new," plan a couple of Success Stories. As you construct your story, use the letters in the word SUCCESS as your guide:

S = Strategic. Make sure your story fits your Agenda. Think about what you want people to know about you or your business, then build your story to teach that point.

U = Unique. Point out what makes you stand out from the crowd. If you're in real estate, for example, don't just say, "I've been selling lots of houses." That's expected. Give a specific and interesting example of a sale. "Last week, I found a home for a couple who both needed home offices. Both of them wanted first floor offices with outside access, lots of light, and great views. I found just the home, one that had two sunny rooms with French doors opening to a patio just off the driveway." This story teaches your conversation partner that you can find the unusual home.

C = Clear. Be sure you eliminate all the jargon of your profession.

C = Concrete. Give a couple of specific details to help your partner see a vivid picture. Those colorful words will stick in the other person's mind more easily than generalities. Notice that you can "see" the home the realtor was describing.

E = *Exciting.* Let your enthusiasm shine through. Use vivid language, an upbeat tone of voice, and a speedy, not draggy, delivery. Make it memorable.

S = *Short and Succinct.* Edit your story to a maximum of 6–10 sentences.

S = *Service-Oriented.* Be sure that your story teaches how well you served the internal or external client, solved the problem, saved the day.

It's a good idea, as you begin to sharpen your storytelling skills, to write out your stories. Then you can throw out the jargon, add vivid details, shorten the length to 6–10 sentences, refocus your stories to make your point or teach something about yourself. Plan Success Stories on several different topics, then use the one that seems most appropriate to the person you are talking with. Carry a notebook with you, so that you can capture ideas for stories. Develop one story a week until finding and telling anecdotes has become a conversational habit you feel confident about. As you are working on this skill, practice your stories on your family.

After you tell your story, ask your conversation partner a question that will elicit his or her story. Our favorite question comes from Ann, who asks, "And what are you excited about these days?"

Sample These Stories

Karen's Story
"I'm working on a project to teach mothers in prison to read to their kids when they come to visit. I work for the Prince Georges County Library System. I teamed up with people in other state agencies to get a grant to teach women inmates at the state prison storytelling skills to use with their pre-schoolers during family visits. I convinced several publishers to donate the books, and it was so much fun to teach the mothers. They really got into making up different voices for the characters in the story. The women loved reading to each other in the practice sessions almost as much as they loved reading to their own children. We had the party yesterday where all the kids came and each child got to take home a book to remember their time with their mom."

So what does Karen's story tell you about her? She knows how to work with others outside the library system. She's good at identifying needs and creating programs to meet them. She's an innovator, a problem-solver. Is her story memorable? Sure!

Lynne's Story

"I just got back from teaching a three-day training course in Seattle. Boy, what a challenge! When I walked into the hotel conference room I noticed that one whole wall was windows overlooking the bay. 'Great room,' I thought to myself. But within the first hour of the class, I could see that my twelve students and I were mesmerized by the bay, longing to be out there. So that evening, I went to the cruise line that sends boats to Victoria and back and said, 'Could I bring twelve people on board tomorrow?' For only a little more money, we had our class on the water for the next two days. We met in a small conference room on board, I brought my flip chart, we worked very hard, and people were delighted to have breaks and lunchtime to stroll around the deck."

So what do you know about Lynne? She's a problem-solver and a leader. She's observant. She's resourceful. She's not willing to put up with an unworkable situation, and she'll go the extra mile to create a good learning environment for her students.

Claire's Story

"I saw the most touching scene last night. I do mediation with couples who are working out custody and financial agreements. The couple I saw on Monday was very hostile and angry. So I just kept providing structure, helping them notice when they found agreement, and reminding them of their goal to stay out of court. The conversation was rocky for at least an hour and then something clicked with them. They left the office, and when I stood up to stretch my legs, I happened to look out the window. There they were, out in the parking lot, hugging. It wasn't a 'Let's get back together' hug. It was more of a 'We can work together for the good of each other and the kids' hug. I was so touched and I thought to myself, 'This is why I do this work.'"

So what did Claire teach you with her story? That she's persistent. That she succeeds even with the most difficult cases. That her work touches her heart.

Allen's Story

"My company, a worldwide consulting firm, is so big that it's hard to know who the experts are. I sent out an e-mail and asked anyone who had a background or an interest in public health to respond. Surprisingly, more than seventy colleagues answered. We formed a Community of Practice. When any one of us is working on a client proposal in that area, it's easy to quickly identify people with specific knowledge. Not only can we tap into their expertise, but we also have an easier time staffing projects. We might ask a specialist to join the team to work with that client. Now I have experts that I can draw on for input when I'm doing client proposals or staffing work. And, of course, everyone else in the CoP knows more about my expertise."

So what do you know about Allen? He takes the initiative to improve the whole organization. He is determined to give clients the best his organization can offer.

People Want to Know . . .

We have taught hundreds of people to tell stories. Here are some of the questions they ask us.

1. *"What if I can't think of any stories?"* Challenge yourself to notice the moments in your life that you'd like to tell others about. Look for experiences in your leisure and professional life that will show who you are. Listen carefully as others tell stories from their lives. Notice that, for the most part, they are talking about everyday events. Don't think you've got to have earthshaking stories—like about a time you rescued someone from a burning building or won a medal at the Olympics. Just look for times that brought out your best or would illustrate your Character and Competence. Keep that notebook with you so you can hang on to your ideas until you get a chance to write them out and edit them.

Ask yourself: "What would I like to teach people about me?" Look back at the goal you set as you read Chapter 5. Would it help you reach your goal if your contacts knew more about your Character and Competence? Do you want people to know that you're a stickler for details? That you're creative? That you're compassionate? That you can be tough when the going gets rough? That you know a lot about designing "green" buildings? Then look for anecdotes that give an example of those things. Figure 11-2 may give you some ideas on how to find your own stories.

2. *"How can I get into my story? When do I tell it?"* Look for a lull in the conversation. Or tell your story in response to "How are you?" or "What's new?" Think of a "transition sentence" that alerts the listener you're about to tell a story. Notice how Claire said, "I saw the most touching scene last night." That's her signal to others that she's going to tell an anecdote.

Here are some other good ideas for transition sentences.

To change the subject when there's a pause in the conversation, say, "I've been meaning to tell you about . . ." or "The most amazing thing happened last week . . ."

FIGURE 11-2. Stories That Make the Point.

What I Want to Teach My Contact	Incident to Base My Story On
Mary: "I pay attention to details."	"How I figured out every possible supply we'd need for a three-day camping trip for eighteen Girl Scouts."
Fred: "I have a sense of humor."	"The jokes I made to keep everyone calm when I was Master of Ceremonies at the awards ceremony and the lights went out."
Donna: "I'm comfortable working with CEOs and celebrities."	"The time I was host to Bill Gates when he visited our model charter school."
Molly: "I'm capable of coping with a crisis."	"The time my boss got sick and I delivered his 30-minute speech to 900 people at the convention."
Weng Po: "I'm a good negotiator and problem-solver."	"How I got the IT and HR departments to collaborate on creating the new employee database."
Mike: "I can handle difficult customers."	"How I won back the business of a disgruntled customer—and increased his order by $75,000."
Lynda: "I go the extra mile for my clients."	"The time I found a partner to cosponsor an ad campaign that was too expensive for my client alone."

To link your anecdote back to a previous conversation, say, "Remember when you told me about working with that client from China? I had a similar experience yesterday that I'd thought you'd be interested in."

To acknowledge your conversation partner's expertise, say, "I know you're a guy who loves the latest high-tech gadgets. Let me tell you about one I used that sure saved the day recently . . ."

To explore your contact's thoughts about an idea you have, say, "You know something interesting happened the other day, and I was curious about what you would think."

To update your contact on new talents or interests you've been developing say, "I had a "first" the other day in my life as a manager. Let me tell you about it."

3. *"What are some tips for shaping my story and making it fun to listen to?"* Relive the moment with relish. Craft your story so it paints a vivid picture. The best stories do several things. They reveal your interests, challenges, and talents so that people have an expanded idea of what to call on you for or what to send your way. And they are memorable enough that the listener could repeat them to others with some degree of accuracy. Ask yourself if you'd want to listen to your story. Practice it several times so you get to the point quickly.

Most stories have a "turnaround"—a moment when you had to do something, come up with a solution, solve a problem. Or a moment when you learned something about yourself or how the world works. Think of the childhood formula for a good story: "Once upon a time . . . Suddenly . . . Luckily . . . Happily ever after." If there's not a "Happily ever after," can you at least point to a lesson learned?

4. *"Won't people think I'm "grandstanding" or "hot-dogging" if I tell a story?"* No. Good conversationalists know how to pepper their conversation with brief, interesting vignettes about who they are and the experiences they've had. Most people won't be there to see your shining moments—how you captured your audience as you spoke at the conference even though the fire alarm went off in the middle of your presentation, or how you survived a camping trip with a dozen eight-year-olds. Think of your story as a gift to the conversation because it offers your conversational partner clues about what topics to bring up next, how to help you, or how to introduce you to others.

"A few years ago," a sports columnist wrote, "I followed Norm Stewart, Missouri's legendary basketball coach, out of a party. He was stopped by ten different people. He made every one of those people feel like the most special person in the world. His secret? He always had a good story to tell."

5. *"What if I accidentally tell my story to the same person twice? Or what if someone overhears me telling the same story? That will be embarrassing!"* Build a collection of stories. Make it a habit to notice moments in your business and leisure life that will make a good anecdote. Figure out how to tell it so that you teach the listener something new about your qualities and skills. Find and tell a new one every week until you have stockpiled enough that you can choose to tell the one that fits the situation or your conversation partner's interests. Jamie has lots of tales to tell that show how she juggles a part-time consulting business and her five-year-old triplets. But those might not be the best stories to tell to clients. She has other stories about getting her pilot's license and about competing on a Masters swimming team that she might tell at a business luncheon to teach about her qualities.

6. *"What if everything I do is classified or I worry about client confidentiality?"* To respect client confidentiality, disguise the particulars or combine several clients' experiences into one to make your story generic.

When Louis asked Cathleen, a CPA, "What's new with you," she said, "One of my clients was upset about a tax penalty for something that happened a couple of years ago. I wrote the most persuasive letter I could devise to the Department of Revenue about the situation. When they backed down and removed the penalty, my client was so relieved."

If your job is top secret, you can still tell stories from your personal life that highlight the qualities that make you special. Or you can genericize your stories from work so that they tell only what you are allowed to reveal.

There are three big conversational skills: generous listening, seriously curious questioning, and strategic storytelling. Master these and you'll be ready to talk to anybody.

CHAPTER 12

End with the Future in Mind

If someone asked you, "What's the most difficult moment in networking?" would you say "Ending the conversation"? Many people do. Introductions and meeting people are stressful, they'll tell you, but at least there's a routine: You shake hands and exchange names. On the other hand, there is no protocol for ending conversations and exiting can often seem awkward.

Prepare for the Next Time

Your Critic may move into high gear when someone—even someone you've made a good connection with—ends a conversation with you. If you are the one doing the leaving, you may feel guilty because it seems as if you are rejecting or abandoning the other person. As a result of these feelings, people say, "I believe I'll freshen my drink," and walk away, not even bothering to head in the direction of the bar. Or they may simply say, with no intention of doing so, "I'll see you later." Or they may drift away when a third person enters the conversation.

To change your mindset about the final moments of a conversation, imagine that you'll continue your dialogue at some time in the future. Always assume that you will see your conversation partner again. Think, "I'm just beginning this relationship. It will be exciting to see it develop." Always prepare for the next time. Making a conscious closing will set the tone for your next meeting.

Listen for the Bell

Tune in to the timetable. There's a bell that goes off in people's minds after a conversation has been going on for about five minutes. At networking events and at many quasi-business gatherings, such as cocktail parties or receptions, people have a vague notion that they should speak with as many people as possible. You will be able to tell from your conversation partner's body language when he is ready to move on. He will look away, gather his possessions, and perhaps even move farther away from you. Notice the bell in your head—your intuitive sense of when it's time to say good-bye.

Eight Ways to Leave

Honesty is rare in the final moments of a conversation, but that's what works best. Be totally honest. Here are eight ways to leave a conversation gracefully and competently with your own integrity—and your contact's—intact.

1. *Center on your Agenda.* Your Agenda will serve you well as you make conscious closings. Saying, "I want . . . I must . . . I need . . ." eliminates the feeling that you are abandoning your conversation partner. Shift the attention to where you are going and the purpose that is motivating you.

Here are some suggestions for closing a conversation by referring to your Agenda:

▶ "I'm going to circulate and welcome some of the new people."

▶ "I need to see three more people before I leave tonight."

▶ "I must speak to the membership chairman before he leaves."

▶ "I want to see if there are any other engineers (or people from my industry, or home-based business people) here."

2. *Ask your contact for a referral.* To change conversation partners, ask your current partner for a referral to someone else in the room. Say:

▶ "I want to find other people who are working at home. Do you know anyone like that?"

▶ "Do you know anyone here who is involved with management training?"

▶ "I'm going to the annual meeting next month. Do you know anybody who went last year?"

▶ "Do you know of anyone who is thinking about moving to a new office this year? My company is expanding its office design services."

3. *Take your contact along with you.* If you feel uncomfortable ending a conversation and walking away from someone, invite that person to go with you:

▶ "Let's see if we can find the registration booth."

▶ "Want a drink? I'm thirsty."

▶ "Would you like to come with me to talk with the new president? I want to ask her about next month's program."

4. *Introduce your contact.* As you look around the room, you may see someone you want to introduce your conversation partner to. Don't think of this as a way to get rid of somebody. Instead, always think, "Who do I know here that my contact might need to meet?"

An example: "Lenora, you mentioned you're going to Vancouver next month. I want to introduce you to Sam. He grew up there and could tell you all about the sights."

Or: "Tom, as soon as Bill arrives, I want to get you two together. Last month you said you were thinking of franchising your stores, and he's a franchise lawyer. I'll bet you two would have a lot to talk about."

5. *Play concentration.* Remember that kids' game where you lay all the cards face down on the table? You turn over a ten of hearts, but you can't have it until you find a match. Your challenge is to remember after several turns where that ten of hearts is.

You can play Concentration in a room full of people, too. You meet Marjory, an interior designer, who specializes in helping seniors downsize and move to smaller quarters. A few minutes later, you talk with Cynthia, who says she's writing a book titled *Moving Mother*. You think to yourself, "I must introduce Cynthia to Marjorie. What a match!" You go out of your way to bring them together. Whether you stay with that conversation or not, they will remember you as a person who knows everybody.

6. *Sum up and appreciate.* One of the most memorable ways to close is to sum up the conversation and show appreciation for your conversation partner. To do that, shake hands and acknowledge the conversation and its importance to you. You could even acknowledge the importance in your life of the relationship you have with your contact that perhaps goes way beyond this encounter. Find a specific quality in the other person or a moment in the conversation that you can genuinely express appreciation for:

▶ "If the other members of ASID are as enthusiastic as you are, I'm going to be very glad I joined."

▶ "Wonderful to see you and to hear about the trade show."

▶ "I'm so glad to know more about your department."

▶ "Thanks for telling me about your new marketing tactics. I'm looking forward to hearing how they are working next month."

7. *Explain the next steps.* Finally, say what you will do next, or what you would like for your contact to do next, to continue the relationship. Many of these suggestions are reassuring to your contact because, in contrast to just melting away, you are being very specific. We call these Magnet Statements because they are designed to pull you back together at some point in the future. They provide the energy to continue the conversation and build the relationship. They signal interest. Let your sincerity shine through. Look the person in the eye. Ask the person for his or her card so you'll have the necessary information to re-connect. Jot a note to yourself on the back of the card while you are still with the person or soon after you part. Say what you will do or what the next step in your relationship will be:

▶ "I'm going to send you that article we talked about."

▶ "This idea really jelled for me when you explained it. I'd like to hear more when we get together."

▶ "I'll ask Jim to call you."

▶ "I'll see you at the next meeting."

▶ "I don't want to monopolize you this evening. Can we arrange to meet later?"

▶ "I hope we can do business after the holidays."

Or ask your contact to follow up:

▶ "Give me a call next week, and we'll set up a time for me to tell you about my publishing experiences. I'm glad you asked me for advice. I'm always eager to help a fellow author. Here's my card."

8. *Shake hands and leave.* After making these final statements, shake hands and leave quickly. No dilly-dallying. Use your body language to emphasize your purposeful leave-taking.

Remember watching a wonderful mini-series? Remember the good feelings of expectation you had when you saw the words "To Be Continued . . ." on the TV screen? That's how you want to leave your contact: Those words hanging in the air, setting the stage for the next episode in your relationship.

A Ritual for Leave-Taking

To close a conversation easily, remember this LEAVE NOW formula:

L = Let go of your conversation partner after five minutes.

E = Explain what you must do. Be honest.

A = Act on your Agenda.

V = Volunteer a referral.

E = Exit easily to another conversation by taking your conversation partner with you.

N = Note what's gone on between you. Sum up the conversation and appreciate something your contact said or did.

O = Outline the next step for your contact.

W = Walk. Shake hands and leave, purposefully.

Do You Have Questions?

Here are some of the questions people have about endings.

Q: "What if I'm talking with someone and we're interrupted?"

A: Look for a way to reconnect before the meeting ends. Mark was listening intently to Susan talk about her expanding business when two other people joined their group and the conversation got sidetracked to another topic. Soon, the chair called the meeting to order. Susan and Mark ended up at different tables. Mark wanted to go on with their conversation because he figured she'd need his office design services sometime in the next year as she added more office space. Before he left the luncheon, he made a point of approaching Susan again, asking for her card, and offering to send her an article he'd written on office lighting.

Q: "What if you really want to keep on talking?"

A: Occasionally, you will find yourself in a conversation that's too good to leave. You want to keep talking with your contact even though the unwritten "rule" says, "Circulate!"

Hal began to talk with Marilyn, the speaker. After five minutes or so, he began to feel uncomfortable because she wasn't having an opportunity to visit with anyone else. Even though they both clearly wanted to continue their conversation, it seemed rude to do so. Finally Hal said, "I don't want to monopolize you. Let's plan to get together sometime in the next month. I'll call so we'll both have our calendars handy."

Q: "I leave events with a pocket full of business cards. I know I should keep and organize the contact information. Got any tips?"

A: You'll keep the contact information for some people because you like their energy or there's good chemistry between the two of you and you want to be on the lookout for ways to continue the relationship. Other cards serve as a reminder that you made a specific commitment that requires Follow Through. And you probably exchanged some cards because you uncovered a commonality or a need that invites further exploration. For instance, when Marilyn and Joe discovered they were both researching which career fairs to attend for their company's college recruitment activities, they had a natural reason to exchange cards.

Put data about people you want to keep track of in your contact management system. This software is a must for the serious networker because it helps you use your contact information in a variety of ways. Before Mike's three-day business trip to Atlanta, he compiled a list of everyone he knows there, so he could decide whom to see. Rochelle called up a list of everyone she'd met last year at her association's annual meeting, so she could refresh her memory about these people before seeing them again this year.

CHAPTER 13

Follow Through

All too often, networkers spend lots of energy making initial contacts and then don't know how to cultivate them so that the relationships pay dividends down the road. Mike, Nancy, and Susan are typical of networkers everywhere. They're trying to figure out how to stay connected. Here's what they say.

"I go to networking events and meet a lot of people and then—nothing happens. What am I doing wrong?" asks Mike, a CPA.

"I talked to a coworker at last month's in-house training session. She's in a division I'd like to transfer to. I can't figure out what to do next. Soon, she'll forget who I am and what we talked about," says Nancy, a middle manager in a Fortune 100 company.

"Bob's company is similar to mine, and I'm sure I could learn a lot from him. Come to think of it, we're doing some advertising that he'd probably like to know about, but I'm not sure what the next step is in getting to know him," says Susan, a sales rep.

Focus on Follow Through

If your networking isn't paying off, give more attention to following through. Follow Through is the act of carrying a motion to its natural completion. Follow Through insures that baseball players and golfers achieve maximum force on the ball. Follow Through insures that you as a networker achieve maximum impact.

Follow Through begins with a good conversation, one in which you Listen Generously and are Seriously Curious to find out what's on your conversation partner's Agenda. A meaty conversation will give you ideas. The best Follow Through is based on the other person's Agenda, not yours.

Ideally, you'll suggest another meeting during that first conversation with someone. You might say, "I'd like to talk with you more about that. How about if I call you on Monday to set up a time to get together?" Say, for example, "I'll give you a call next month so that we can get together for lunch." You'll want to set up a chain reaction of six to eight encounters to establish a networking relationship. You won't have to initiate every meeting. You know you'll see Tom at the next task force meeting, for example, and you'll reconnect with Clara at the board meeting.

Figure Out Your Reasons to Reconnect

Why *do* you want to get back in touch? Here are three great reasons.

1. *Chemistry.* You like the person and you can imagine because of what he does (chairs the diversity task force, for instance), who he knows (people in Seattle where you plan to move next year), the experiences he's had (worked in London), that it will be mutually beneficial if you have the time to teach and learn and explore together.

2. *Commitment.* You had a rich, Agenda-based conversation that requires some specific next step. You promised to provide a phone number or website or piece of information.

3. *Commonality.* You found you have something in common or uncovered a need that begs to be explored.

Face Your Fears

Do you feel uncomfortable about taking that first step to reestablish a dialogue—especially if quite a bit of time has elapsed since you met with your contact?

Rob handles that problem like this. He calls and asks, "Isn't it about time for our annual lunch?"

Maybe it hasn't been a year, but you're still afraid that the person you'd like to re-connect with won't remember you. You could ask a colleague or friend to re-introduce you.

You have a good reason to reconnect. You'd like to build a relationship because you think the person would be useful to you and perhaps you could help him, too. But that probably feels like far too much to ask for initially. People tell us they'd feel more comfortable if they had "an excuse" for calling or setting up another encounter. But when you think of follow up as Follow Through, you don't need an "excuse." Follow Through becomes a legitimate, integral, natural *completion* of the process, not an add-on or afterthought.

Reconnecting does become more comfortable when you re-open a conversation by reminding your contact of something you have in common. These ideas will help your contact remember you.

Refer back to when and how you met. "We met in that computer course a couple of weeks ago. Are you using the software they suggested? I've figured out some tricks I'll be glad to show you."

Refer to a common need. "Since we're both starting businesses, I was interested in what you said about looking for office space. I'm working on that, too. How about getting together to talk about strategy?"

Refer to proximity. "We work near each other; let's get together for lunch." Or, "We live in the same neighborhood, let's meet at the deli for supper next week." Or, "We sat at the same table at the Chamber of Commerce dinner. I'd like to know more about the sales training program you mentioned."

Refer to a common background. "I noticed that we both went to the University of Florida. I got a flyer saying there's going to be an alumni get-together to watch the game next week. Do you want to go?" Or, "Don't you have a degree in English, too? I'd be very interested to know how you made the transition to PR. How about coffee later this week?"

Appreciate your contact's contributions. "You're doing a great job heading up the program committee. I did that for the Des Moines chapter, and I know what a big job it is. We developed a great checklist for planning any event. If you think your committee members could use it, I'll drop it by your office."

Refer to a common acquaintance. "You know Burt, don't you? When I talked with him, he suggested we get together. I'm heading up the fundraiser for the hospital. Burt said you did one last year and might be able to give me some pointers. How about breakfast next week?"

Refer to time or money savers. "I heard you say you're feeling overwhelmed with paperwork. I was too, so I hired an office organizer. I'd be happy to share some of her tips with you. They helped me completely overhaul my office. Would you like to come over and see what I did?"

Fill in the Blanks on Your Calendar

Set a goal for the number of networking calls and meetings you want to do every week. When you are planning your week, pull out your calendar and schedule your networking. Don't just think about it, do it.

When people decide to create an active network of 50 to 250 or more contacts, they worry about how much time it will take. It takes less time than you might think.

Dean and Marta's Story

Dean and Marta met at a luncheon meeting of their professional group. As entrepreneurs, they were always looking for work. They shared many common interests and friends. They were very clear with each other about their goals. He said, "I'm a career coach for lawyers who want to reassess their career options." She said, "I teach executives how to handle high-stakes press conferences." Their networking is practically effortless because they both know what the other has to give and wants to find. As you look at their interactions over a period of one year, you can see that Dean and Marta spent only about three hours networking with each other during that time.

February: Marta sent Dean a news article telling about an upcoming, one-week course for lawyers on career changing issues. Dean followed up and was invited to be a guest speaker.

April: Dean called Marta with the name of a law firm looking for a motivational speaker. Marta passed the lead on to a speaker who had referred an executive client to her.

May: Marta and Dean had lunch, updated each other on recent successes and challenges, and enjoyed each other's company.

September: Marta referred her lawyer cousin to Dean for career counseling.

December: Dean and Marta chatted at a holiday party. Marta told Dean she was looking for clients in Europe. Dean introduced Marta to a lawyer he knew who had recently returned after spending a year in London.

It's not the amount of time, but the quality of the interaction that counts in networking.

The Five Goals of Follow Through

What are you trying to achieve as you nurture networking relationships? Take another look at the Rate Your Relationships quiz in Chapter 4. Notice how relationships develop. Aim for these five goals as you stay in touch.

Teach your contacts:

1. Your name and how to reach you easily.

2. Exactly what you do.

3. To have faith in your ability to serve or supply them—or people they refer to you—expertly.

4. What kinds of clients, customers or job opportunities you are seeking and what you can refer to them.

5. What kind of information and opportunities you are looking for.

As you reach these goals with your contacts, you will begin to—and continue to—reap the benefits of networking.

Freshen Up Your Relationships

A businessperson said to us, "I realized that I don't make enough phone calls—general how-are-you, was-just-wondering-how-things-are-going, stay-in-touch type calls—to people in my network. I think I'm afraid the call is going to take too much time—too much of my time, too much of their time. Part of the problem is I'm not sure how to end the call. Any suggestions or thoughts on how I can call more and stress less?"

Before you call, think of three things to say to your contact. You speak at about the rate of 150 words per minute so even in a three-minute call you can say quite a bit. Remember networking is about teaching, so every conversation, whether face-to-face or by phone, is a chance to teach. Here are three ideas for your phone call Agenda.

1. Come up with a bit of information that verifies that you know who your contact is and what he is interested in. "You know, I was thinking about you the other night when we had dinner at a Korean restaurant. I was remembering the stories you told about trying all the delicacies when you were living in Seoul. I wasn't quite that brave."

2. Have something to give. "You'd mentioned your job was requiring more and more in the way of negotiating skills. I just heard that there's a speaker on that very topic at the Wharton Alumni Club Tuesday night—would you like to be my guest?"

3. Think of a Success Story that teaches your contact something about your interests and your expertise. "My job has taken an interesting turn: I'm not only writing the speeches for the executives, I'm now coaching them on their presentation skills—something that requires a great deal of tact!"

When you get your contact on the phone, ask, "Is this a good time to talk for a couple of minutes?"

As you chat, listen for new information about what might be on his or her Agenda so you can respond generously, either by giving some useful information immediately or sending some information later. Or listen for a topic to talk about when you next meet. A good question to get your contact to talk is to ask, "What have you been working on lately?"

To end the call, talk about the next step for your relationship. If this is a person you want to see on a regular basis, build that idea into your comment. "Let's have our quarterly lunch in late September."

Find the Way

As you decide how you will Follow Through, here are some of the things you'll need to consider. Do you want face time or can you use the written word or electronic communication? Do you want to become visible to only one person or many people at the same time? How much time can you afford to spend? What's your budget? As you choose your method, take these tactical tradeoffs into account. Balance the time or money each method takes with its potential for building the relationship. Then decide which way is right for you, with a particular contact, in a particular situation. Follow Through ideas come in all flavors. Choose from among these thirty ideas—one for every day in the month.

1. *Share a cab.* Split the cab fare as you go to a meeting or event.

2. *Park and walk.* Park your car in a new spot in the company parking lot every day and chat with a different person as you walk into the building.

3. *Lend a book.* Deliver a book or CD you have enjoyed to a contact. As you visit, ask about projects that person is working on and be ready to tell about your latest successes and challenges.

When Mike met Charles at a Rotary International luncheon, Charles said, "I'm on the library's waiting list for that business bestseller." Mike asked for his business card and said, "I have a copy. I'll give you a call and bring it over to you."

4. *Forward the freebies.* Provide access to events, people, and resources – dinner with a visiting author, your library of training DVDs, a sneak preview of a movie, tickets to a sports event, or speech.

5. *Pull up a chair.* At a meeting or event, plan to sit next to someone you'd like to know better. Call your contact before the event and say, "Hey, we haven't had a chance to talk for a while. Let's sit together at the luncheon and catch up."

6. *Have a bunch to lunch.* Ask a few people you'd like to know better to lunch. Pick your lunch bunch carefully so that the benefits of their becoming better acquainted with you and with each other are obvious. Marcella, who owns a small advertising agency, frequently invites a mix of clients and potential clients to a catered lunch in her conference room. "They seem to enjoy meeting each other. Often, the stories my current clients tell to my potential clients 'sell' them on using my services."

7. *Tip the talkers.* Before a meeting begins, chat with the speaker or emcee. Let that person know what interests you about the topic and your experience with it. Presenters appreciate knowing more about their audiences. A mention of you from the podium acts almost like an endorsement and certainly gives you more visibility and credibility.

Fred, the owner of a franchise sign shop, gave other attendees a ready-made way to Follow Through with him after the presentation. He showed up early at a workshop on marketing and talked to the speaker. When she asked about his work, he said, "I make signs and banners for all kinds of businesses. I also do a complete range of signs that comply with Americans With Disabilities Act regulations." When a workshop participant asked about the ADA signage regulations, the speaker said, "Fred's company has done a lot of that. Fred, stand up, so people will be able to find you during our coffee break."

8. *Find someone to thank.* Late Friday afternoon, when not much else is going on, look back over your week and find five people to thank. Karishma sent a funny card to Elena, a coworker who'd tutored her on the new software. Mike shot an e-mail to Bill thanking him for a referral. Jane ordered a gift basket of coffee and specialty chocolates for the three people who supported her the most during her successful job search. Mary made a phone call to Stan, appreciating his advice on companies who would reliably handle the office move she was managing.

9. *Host a meeting.* Want to show some influential people where your business is located and give them a clear image of what you do? Offer to have the committee or board meeting at your place. To make your business real to attendees, give a quick guided tour. Talk informally about awards on the wall, new equipment, new capabilities, and various services you provide.

10. *Extend an invitation.* Want to see someone more frequently? Encourage your contact to visit and perhaps join an organization you already belong to.

11. *Speak out.* Speak to the local chapter of an association. Provide a news release to your local newspaper or business publication about the program. Send that same news release to contacts you think might be interested in the topic and ask them to let you know if they will attend. Be sure to say hello, and Follow Through with a note saying, "Nice to see you."

12. *Throw a party.* Invite contacts to your place of business to give people a better idea of what you do. If you work at home, team up to find an interesting place for your open house. Select your co-host carefully. Look for someone with whom you might have customers in common.

Artist Carol works at home, so she teamed up with frame shop owner, Kari, to showcase both businesses with an after hours wine and cheese party. She and Kari invited both past and potential customers to view Carol's drawings and to see Kari's frames.

13. *Add food.* You can extend almost any activity by adding a meal or a cup of coffee at the end. That gives you time to talk. After the soccer practice, plan a picnic. After the training session at work, go out for a drink or coffee.

Sue had met several women at the health club, but they didn't usually have time for extended conversation. That's when she came up with the Breakfast Bunch. The group meets for breakfast one Saturday a month after they exercise.

14. *Honor the volunteers.* Have you enlisted volunteers for your favorite charity? Bring them together.

Wendie's final project for her graduate degree was designed to encourage eleven-year-old girls to think about careers in science and to provide role models for them. She invited her contacts—professional women in scientific areas—to help with the project. After the project was over, she invited the women to a "dutch treat" celebration brunch at a local restaurant to introduce them to each other.

15. *Drop by.* Turner wrote a letter to his franchise training director recommending Gloria, a speaker, for the next training conference and sent her a copy. Rather than calling to say thanks, Gloria dropped by Turner's store. She said, "Your letter was wonderful. I appreciated it so much. I will follow up with the training director. Do you have time to give me the grand tour of your store and to tell me about your products and services? I want to understand exactly what you and your fellow franchisees do before I make a proposal to the training director. And want to be able to recommend you to anyone I run into who needs printing."

16. *Face it.* When face-to-face contact isn't feasible, send your face. Have a note card that fits into a business envelope printed up with your photo on it.

17. *Send a postcard.* Out of town on business or vacation? Take some addresses with you. Buy a handful of postcards, or before you go, have postcards printed with your picture, your logo, a saying that makes people think of your service or product, or some interesting facts about your industry. Write a note confirming a future meeting with your contact.

When Ron (a professional speaker and humorist) travels for business, he always takes a stack of the postcards he had specially designed so he can mail notes to prospects and clients. Ron's postcard shows him standing in front of a huge hotel ballroom full of rows and rows of empty seats. The caption under Ron's big smile says, "Wish you were here!"

18. *Notice publicity.* Peruse the newspaper watching for publicity about any of your contacts. Clip articles and send them with sticky notes. Or cut out your contact's advertisements and send with a note telling what made the ad leap off the page and grab your attention.

19. *Get feedback.* Ask your contact to review something you've written. Tom writes a short column each month for his professional association magazine. As a supplier of services that members often need, he finds it an excellent way to establish his credibility and name recognition in his specialized marketplace. About three weeks before his deadline, he sends his column to a couple of prospects, clients, or referral sources and asks for their comments, suggestions, and a reality check. They are honored to be seen as a sounding board and often have good examples or suggestions.

20. *Send the news.* If your business involves providing information—and who's doesn't?— produce a print or electronic newsletter or blog. Highlight your successes, new products and services. Show how clients or customers benefit. Help your contacts see how they could use your expertise. Quoting or featuring customers also enhances your credibility and testifies to your Character and Competence.

21. *Provide a calendar.* Send your contact a calendar of events you'll be involved in or clients you will be working with. This idea works well for musicians, artists, trainers, consultants, craftspeople, speakers, and freelancers, for example.

22. *Give a goodie.* Send your contact a bagel and cream cheese or a couple of donuts—or even a single, specialty tea or coffee bag—along with some information you'd like that person to take time to look at. Notice that this technique "creates" a coffee and bagel break in your contact's day for her to focus on your information.

23. *Announce your news.* Get the word out about an achievement, a move, or a promotion. Send a news release, postcard, or note. This is a good way to teach contacts about your Competence.

24. *Read all about it.* Send your contacts an article that mentions you as an expert. If you haven't been in the news recently, send an article that gives information on the kind of service or product you provide. That way, you can "piggyback" on an article in the news media, positioning yourself as an expert.

Jim's firm analyzes overhead costs for small and mid-sized businesses. When The Wall Street Journal featured an article on rising overhead costs for small businesses, he sent copies, with a personal note and his brochure to twenty potential clients.

25. *Wish 'em a happy.* Send a card on an unusual holiday—Fourth of July, your birthday, Labor Day—to avoid having your message become just one of many at the end of the year. Or send birthday cards to contacts on their birthdays.

26. *Be a winner.* Entering a professional association awards program takes time and effort, but if you win, it's worth it. All the reviewers who evaluate the entries learn of your expertise. Whether you win or not, send a thank you note to each of them.

27. *Delegate responsibility.* Make a list of people you want to stay in touch with and have your assistant send a short, personal message, drafted by you, every couple of months.

28. *Create a quiz.* Design a quiz to teach people about your product or service. Put the quiz on a wallet-sized card to give out to potential clients or distribute it by fax, mail, or e-mail.

Jeff, who owns a carpet store, created a quiz: "Do You Know How to Buy Carpet?" When he meets someone who is thinking about buying carpet, he says, "Give me your business card, and I'll send you my quiz. It will help you know what to look for as you make your decision. Of course, I hope you'll come by my store as you are shopping."

29. *Give yourself a job.* Find a reason to interview your contact. Gene was on the planning committee for the next regional conference for his professional association. When he met Melissa, he asked her if he could interview her about what she'd like to see on the program. Andie was putting together a proposal for an employee survey. She asked if she could talk with Margi about "lessons learned" from the survey Margi's company had done last year.

30. *Add to their library.* Give contacts a copy of a book you have written or a book that relates to the product or service you provide. One key idea in Following Through is to provide something to contacts that they will keep a long, long time, so that your name and phone number are available and visible for a long, long time. Giving a book accomplishes just that.

Bonus: Five More Ingenious Ways to Fit In Follow Through

You can do networking on the run. Use bits and pieces of time effectively. Make multitasking a way of life. Notice that all of these ideas allow you to network as you are doing something you already have on your calendar or to-do list.

1. *Piggyback.* Have coffee with a contact after the meeting or get to the event early so you can talk with the movers and shakers.

2. *Enlist a volunteer.* Ask a contact to join you in a charitable activity like Habitat for Humanity, so that you see her more frequently.

3. *Share a sandwich.* Rather than sitting with your usual group, ask someone in another department to have lunch with you in the company cafeteria.

4. *Sweat together.* Ask a contact to join you for a walk or a bike ride.

5. *Take to the skies.* Flying to a conference? Call a contact and arrange to sit next to each other on the plane.

PART IV

Select Your Settings

Where will you use your networking skills?

▶Inside your corporation, non-profit, government agency? Here are the tools you need to assess and navigate the complexity of your workplace culture. You'll get state-of-the-art tactics that will show you the best ways to create your network at work.

▶To develop business? You can professionalize your practice development. You'll find out how to make it rain clients.

▶As you work at home? You'll learn how to connect as you go it alone.

▶In various networking venues, such as professional associations or Chambers of Commerce? You'll find out how to select the best organizations for your purposes and how to make the most of your memberships.

▶In referral groups? You'll discover how to get the most out of relationships in your group.

▶At conventions? You'll see how to get the information, inspiration, and—most important—the interaction you came for.

►As you job hunt? You'll be able to use the special networking skills most job-hunters don't know about to find the perfect job faster or leap from one career field to another.

Whatever the setting, you'll find cutting-edge ideas in these chapters that will help you advance your career as you put your portfolio of networking skills to work in the world.

CHAPTER 14

Network at Work

No matter where you work—a corporation, government agency, university, association, non-profit, or other kind of organization— networking is a pivotal professional competency. It's the BEST way to get the job done, make things work, improve the processes, and advance your career.

Got the Right Word?

Recognize that in some organizations the word "networking" makes people uncomfortable. Don't be fooled. A lot of networking is no doubt going on, but under the alias of "relationship building," "teamwork," "collaboration," "social acumen," "connectivity," "social capital," 'horizontal integration," "inclusion," "collaborative knowledge networks," or "communities of practice." Check your own organizational initiatives for hints that relationship building is a corporate priority.

Bank On the Benefits

Professors from the nation's top business schools (e.g., Harvard, Wharton, Kellogg) are writing articles touting the benefits and necessity of networking at work. Their research substantiates what we've found as we've worked to support all kinds of organizations as they teach employees how to network. Relationship building has become a corporate priority, and yet people are not sure how to go about making it part of the corporate culture. Interestingly, no one department or function has claimed "ownership" of networking in most organizations. No one area has "championed" or "sponsored" an organization-wide approach. The time is right for all the stakeholders to get together and coordinate their plans to advance networking as a core competency. The stakeholders might logically include marketing, business development, career development, mentoring programs, leadership and employee development programs, corporate communications, human resources, executive coaching, affinity groups, and diversity programs, etc. Who in your organization recognizes and teaches networking as a skill-set everybody needs?

The benefits of networking outweigh the efforts. Persuade the powers that be that networking is vital to the health of your organization. And clarify networking's benefits to your organization and to you.

Networking at work helps you to:

▶ *Keep getting the big picture.* Things change fast. Use your network to keep up with what's going on. What percent of sales in your organization are from products or services that didn't exist five years ago? Employees have to stay on their toes, just to know what products their company makes. To remind yourself of the rate of change in your workplace, take a look at the last few issues of your company's annual report.

▶ *Bolster the bottom line.* Understand that your job depends on the success of the organization. Look around for ways to link up efforts to produce income. Sherman facilitated internal strategic planning sessions at the bank. He realized that offering help with strategic planning to non-profits might attract them to bring their business to the bank. He asked himself, "What other things might these organizations need?" He enlisted people from several other departments to provide clients and prospects with a package of services.

▶ *Venture into the white spaces.* Look at the organization chart. What do you see? Boxes linked by some vertical lines that indicate the chain of command? Now, look between the boxes. What do you see? White space? In most organizations, that white space is unexplored territory for networking. That's where you'll find the unmet needs, the undiscovered problems, the opportunities, and the connections that will enhance your career and allow you to contribute more to the organization's success.

An enterprising government employee in Fairfax County, VA, made a list of all languages spoken by employees in various departments so they could serve their increasingly diverse customers better. Her willingness to venture out into the white space helped her showcase her skills and get a better job. It was a win for the county, a win for the citizens, and a win for her.

▶ *Uncork bureaucratic bottlenecks.* If you create temporary project teams to tackle problems and launch initiatives, you'll make a name for yourself. Increase collaboration with other departments.

Patricia used her internal network to change an operational policy that was causing difficulties for people in several departments every quarter. She talked with a key contact in the operations department to find out the history and exact intent of the current policy. Her contact suggested that she talk with two managers who had strong feelings about the policy. She interviewed those managers to determine their concerns. She researched and drafted her policy amendment. Then she consulted with two of her peers to see if they had any additional information she should consider. She also wanted to gain their support for her proposal. One of them told her about some recent legal developments that she was unaware of.

Without her network, Patricia might have created an unacceptable proposal. With her network, she was able to gather the information and feedback she needed, while building support among key people for the amendment. Her policy change was accepted.

Any time you are working on something that will affect people outside your own department, take the time to "field test" your idea. That way, you'll build support for the idea because you've included others in the process. "No surprises" is a cardinal rule of corporate life. Pre-testing ideas prevents surprises.

▶ *Expand your knowledge base.* Figure out what resources you need and put together a network made up of people representing many different interests and areas of expertise. If you introduce your contacts to each other, you can encourage information and skill sharing among all the members of the group. As you network, you expose yourself to new ideas and ways of doing things. This "cross pollination" almost always benefits the organization.

▶ *Create your safety net.* Take responsibility for your own career self-management. Network to increase your visibility within your organization so that opportunities find you! Explore options in case your job goes away. In these days of rightsizing and restructuring, it's smart to keep your ears open. Ask yourself, "What skills do I have that could be used in other areas of the organization?" Figure out how to showcase those skills. What can you do so that others become aware of your capabilities?

Maria offered to manage the 10-K run for a local charity. Sue noticed how much the community sponsors liked working with her and how well-organized she was. When a job opened up in Sue's department, she thought of Maria.

Gary wanted to move from a technical area into training. When line managers were invited to teach a career management course, Gary volunteered. He was able to brush up on training skills as he took the train-the-trainer course and to showcase his teaching skills as he presented the career course. When the training department was looking for a technical trainer, Gary's name came up and he was able to make the switch.

▶ *Access inside information.* Through networking you can get information before it is public. And that information comes with the evaluation and insight your contact adds—something you'll never get from an official announcement.

▶ *Develop a power base.* In organizations, power comes from being an information broker—someone who can stimulate collaboration among many different groups and make things happen. This power has nothing to do with your place on the organization chart.

▶*Round up talent.* Put together a circle of contacts with diverse skills that broaden your ability to get things done and insure the success of your projects and initiatives.

Ten Ways to Get on Board Quickly

Got a new job? It may take you as many as six months to feel that you are in control of your job. When your orientation takes that long, your organization loses the ability to tap into your creativity, knowledge, new perspectives, expertise, industry contacts, and fresh ideas.

What can you do to leap into the saddle ASAP? Here are ten ideas. Notice how many of them deal with building an internal network! You'll learn how to do that in the rest of this chapter.

1. Recognize that you, in a new situation, will need to notice the cultural ground rules and be aware of some of the organizational history before leaping into action.

2. Know that most organizations think that providing you with information is the key to helping you become productive quickly.

3. Get clear that your best strategy is to build relationships, not gulp information. The more connected you feel, the more you'll feel satisfied and committed to your new job.

4. Often introductions to others in an organization aren't strategic and are done during a quick walk down a hallway. Ask your boss, "Who do I need to get to know?" Say, "When you introduce me, I know you'll be telling about my background. It will help me out if you'll also fill me in on the other person's roles and projects. That way, it will be easier for me to go back later and delve into things I need to get up to speed on."

5. Ask for or select on your own a "buddy of the week" for at least your first month on the job. This will give you someone to ask questions of.

6. Ask questions and engage in conversations in which you explore your co-workers' and subordinates' abilities, skills,

and knowledge. Talk to people about their roles and re-sponsibilities.

7. Take advantage of your newbie "halo." When you begin, you have a window of time in which people expect you to be a bit different. Even if networking is not the norm in your organization, you can use this time to get out of your cubicle and meet as many people as you can.

8. Ask for assignments that bring you in contact with others, not stand-alone projects.

9. Jump over to other groups and find out how your group and theirs are connected.

10. Identify the in-house experts and resource people. Ask everyone you talk with, "Who else should I get to know?" When the same names keep popping up, you will have found the key influencers. Call and arrange to meet. Ask your boss to contact these folks in advance of your call so you are never "calling cold."

Assess Your Corporate Culture

If you've decided that you need to work on your network, begin by assessing your corporate culture. Is your organization network-friendly? To determine how supportive your workplace is, ask yourself these questions:

▶Do corporate initiatives mention relationship building in any way? If so, there is recognition at the top that building "social capital" is valuable.

▶Is training offered? You can suggest networking workshops or suggest that the skills be embedded in existing leadership or employee development training.

▶Are you encouraged to belong to professional associations and to attend both monthly meetings and conferences?

▶Are you encouraged to volunteer in the community, serve on boards, etc.?

▶Is it easy—and expected—for you to collaborate with people in other departments—to venture out into the white space on the organizational chart?

▶How much money will your organization spend on professional association dues and conferences for you? Collateral expenses, such as travel, lodging, etc.? Is anyone tracking whether the organization is getting its money's worth?

▶Are networking activities/goals included in your annual performance plan?

▶Are you rewarded when your networking contributes to the success of the organization?

Recognize that in some organizations, networking violates the cultural ground rules. If that's your assessment, talk with your boss and your colleagues about the reasons for networking inside your organization. Use ideas from this chapter to convince them that networking at work pays off—for the organization and for the individual.

Some forward-thinking organizations are deliberately working to create a more collaborative culture by setting up mentoring programs, encouraging the formation of communities of practice, sponsoring women's networks and other affinity groups, and providing ways for people to interview others to discuss lateral moves and opportunities for upward mobility.

Even if you've decided that your organization's culture isn't very network-friendly, you'll still find ideas in this chapter that will work for you. Focus not on self-serving objectives, but on serving internal and external customers, streamlining internal processes, getting the job done, and impacting the bottom line.

How Strong Is Your Inside Network?

Use this quiz to rate the strength of your current inside network.

1. Do you know people at all levels of the organization? Do they know your name and what you do?

2. Do you know all the people whose work intersects yours in any way?

3. Do you know people who have jobs you might like to have some day?

4. Are you involved in any cross-functional efforts or interdepartmental activities (e.g., temporary assignments, committees, task forces, special projects, volunteer activities)?

5. Are you plugged into the grapevine? Do you find out what's up before your boss tells you?

6. Do you take every opportunity to meet face-to-face to define and discuss complex problems, shifting priorities, areas of responsibility?

7. Do you know and talk with others about tools to get the job done today and trends that will impact your job in the future?

8. Do you have effective internal channels through which to send information?

9. When you see a problem that involves people from various areas, do you take the initiative to bring people together to solve it?

10. Do you drop by to see people—even when you don't need anything?

Could you say "Yes" to most of those questions? If not, make building your inside network a priority.

Map Out a Plan

Draw a map of your contacts. On a big piece of paper, draw a circle and put your name in it. Then draw circles with the names of everyone at work that you interact with. Add circles with the names of everyone you think you should interact with. If you don't know the name of one of these people, use his or her title or describe the type of job he or she has. For example, you may decide you want to know the editor of the corporate newsletter or someone in the IT department who can troubleshoot problems. You can find out those people's names later. Who else do you want or need to know in order to solve problems, contribute to the bottom line, uncork bottlenecks, and create career security? This map is your current and potential network at work.

On your map, rate each relationship:

Write *E* next to the name of any person with whom you believe you have a positive, mutually beneficial relationship.

Write *R* next to the name of any person with whom you believe you have a negative, unpleasant, or unproductive relationship.

Write *S* next to the name of any person with whom you have no relationship or a neutral relationship.

(STOP: DO NOT READ ANY FURTHER UNTIL YOU HAVE MADE YOUR MAP!)

You may be amazed as you take a few minutes and analyze your map.

Where is your circle? At the center of the page? At the top? How big is your circle compared to the other circles? Do they vary in size? Did you connect all the other circles to your own with lines? Did you arrange the other people's circles in any way? You may gain some insights about the "distance" you perceive between you and other people by this analysis. What else can you discover about your network? Do you have a lot of *S* ratings? What does that tell you? Are there lots of circles without names?

ENHANCE, START, or REPAIR your relationships.

Next create your strategic plan to increase the breadth of your network, the strength of your network, and the effectiveness of your network.

Using your map, make a list of everyone who has a *E* by his or her name. Begin with this group. The next time you get together with one of these people, take the opportunity to mention the way you have worked together—the problems you've solved, the processes you've improved, the projects you've collaborated on. Remind the person of milestones in the history of your relationship—how you met, what you have done for each other, your successes—even your failures. Say how much you appreciate that person. Let him know you want to continue your relationship and to **ENHANCE** it. Verbalize your trust in that person and your reliance on that person's expertise. Ask for his or her help and offer your help. You don't have to be specific. Say, "I know I can count on you to brainstorm with me when I need a good idea. You know you can always call on me for help." Use this meeting to confirm your relationship. Resolve to consistently be on the lookout for ways to contribute to that person's success and to stay in touch on a regular basis—even when you don't need anything. You might want to suggest that you have lunch once a month, for example.

Next, make a list of everyone who has a *S* by his or her name. Choose someone on the list and come up with a concrete reason to **START** getting together. You might say, for example, "I'd like to work with you to streamline this process. I'd like to explore how we could cut several days out of the processing time." Or, if you are thinking about your career, you might say, "Long-term, I'd like to make a move from my staff position to one that has more impact on the bottom line. I'd like to know how you did it." Remember that to get, you must give. As you become acquainted, listen for that person's workplace goals and challenges so that you can contribute. Listen Generously so that you can give more than you receive. Take every opportunity to be helpful. Understand that you will need to meet, face-to-face, with the person six to eight times to build a mutually trusting and beneficial relationship. Trust is built on an appreciation of the other person's Character and Competence. Put those meetings on your calendar over a period of six months or so. Supplement those meetings with e-mail and phone calls.

Finally, ask yourself what's going on with the relationships you rated *R*. If one of these relationships involves a person you absolutely must work effectively with, make it priority to **REPAIR** that situation. "But," you may be saying to yourself, "You don't know Joe—he's impossible!" Or, "Nobody could work with Kayla!" It's true. Sometimes you must deal with difficult people. And sometimes, sticky situations and shrinking resources can make even the nicest people hard to get along with. If that's the case, see the situation as an opportunity to develop your own influencing skills. Get a copy of *The Empowered Manager: Positive Political Skills at Work*, by Peter Block. Learn his system for cultivating Allies and for limiting the negative impact of Adversaries, Opponents, Bedfellows and Fence-Sitters. Block would suggest meeting with the problem person and saying something like this: "In the past, we've had conflicts. I'd like to change that, so that when we work together it's positive and productive. Let's talk about how we can overcome the past and start fresh." Suggest "ground rules" for how you'll work together in the future. You might say, "When you see a problem, come to me first, rather than talking to Sue and Bill and Wang." Or, "If your people are running behind by more than thirty-six hours, let me know so we can adjust things here." Over time, you may or may not be able to improve the relationship or even get the project back on track, but your sense of confidence and your reputation as a relationship builder will grow. If you have tried to change the nature of your interactions without success, give it up as a lost cause and spend your time and energy connecting with someone who is more amenable to working with you.

Pair Up with Peers

Besides networking with the people your job intersects with, it's valuable to exchange information with your peers, people at your own level throughout your organization. Jerry, who worked in the corporate planning department, happened to sit down at the same lunch table with Marcia, who was the corporate speechwriter. He told her about his involvement with the school district where he lived. She said she'd just written a speech for the chairman of the board on education and knew that he was very interested in finding a way to support projects like the one Jerry was working on. She suggested that Jerry talk with the chairman about corporate funding for the project. Jerry did and was tapped to head up the corporation's efforts with educational institutions.

Your peers can provide support for you outside your own work group. They can give you information that is vital to your career. And they can increase your visibility in the organization.

Avoid Erroneous Assumptions

Know the rules. Here are eight erroneous assumptions to avoid as you network at work.

1. "People I work with are automatically part of my network." Not true. You must create and nurture the relationships.

2. "Everyone is an equally good networking contact." Not true. Seek out the experts, the influencers, and people who will

give back. As you talk with people in your network, agree to respond quickly to their requests.

3. "It's his job to give me information. I shouldn't have to 'make nice' to get it." Not true. You'll get better help faster when you are obviously willing to help. Listen Generously to your contact. Does that person need something you can supply? If you can't discover anything, ask, "How can I help you?"

4. "Since we work at the same organization, I can access anyone." Not true. The "best" contacts are busy people. Use referrals, references, and introductions by a third party. And become known for the people you connect.

5. "I don't have to prepare like I would for an external contact, since we're colleagues." Not true. Don't waste your contact's time. Before you ask for something, do as much study or research as possible. That will provide you with some basic information. Jot down what you've found as you've tried to solve the problem or find the out-of-the-ordinary information. Note any blind alleys you discovered. Form your question(s) carefully. Make your quest interesting and intriguing for your contact. Link your question or need to something of interest to your contact. That way, you're not just asking for a handout. Is there a payoff for him or her? Try to find one. If you can't, be sure you volunteer to be helpful.

6. "My request is so important that my contact will drop everything to answer it yesterday." Not true. Make sure you give your contact enough time. If you need something, don't procrastinate. Ask early, before you are desperate.

7. "When I receive the information, the interaction is over." Not true. Get back in touch to tell your contact "the rest of the story," and what use you made of what he or she gave you.

8. "I said, 'Thanks.' That should be enough." Not true. Size your "Thank you" to match the size of the favor. Send a handwritten note. Take your contact out to lunch. Send a funny card. Write a note to your contact's boss. Take every opportunity to give credit publicly.

Overcome the Barriers

Yes, there are barriers in most organizations. Old hierarchies and ways of doing things linger on, even after executive pronouncements that give employees "permission" to network. And you may have some beliefs that make networking challenging for you. Here are some questions—and answers—that may help.

Q: "I do a good job. Shouldn't my work stand on its own? Do I really have to 'promote' myself?"

A: In an ideal world, your work would be noticed and appreciated. But in the real world, you must make your good work visible. It's often true that people who are promoted most often and get the biggest salary increases are not necessarily the most technically competent, but are those who are willing to make their competence visible.

Q: "I don't think networking is 'the thing to do' here. But I can see the benefits. Any ideas for a first step?"

A: Talk with your coworkers in the department and, when you are sure you have their support, enlist your boss in a low-risk, high-payoff activity, like a brown-bag lunch with another department. When the corporate communications department at a telecommunications company invited the human resources department to lunch, it was the beginning of a rich collaboration. As people got to know each other, they integrated their strategic planning so that an HR request for the production of a training calendar was on the corporate communications department's annual schedule. If you collaborate, you can negotiate to even out the workload, so all the projects don't hit at the same time.

Q: "I'm okay networking with peers, but I freeze up when I have to talk to the higher-ups. How can I be more comfortable?"

A: Get in touch with your Agenda. Is it something you would not want as a headline in tomorrow's newspaper? "I want to snow this person. I want him to like me better than my colleague, so that I'll get a promotion." That's a hidden Agenda. There's a small, but significant difference in an up-front Agenda you could legitimately make conversation from. Say, "I want to clearly demonstrate in this conversation the level of my expertise about this subject to my boss," or "I want my fundraising skills to be visible, so I'm a natural candidate for the new venture."

Q: "Won't talking with higher ups be seen as bootlicking or grandstanding?"

A: If you sincerely and openly network with everyone in your organization—your work group, your subordinates, and your peers, not just people above you in the organization—you will feel more comfortable. That kind of openness will become your way of operating in the organizational environment. Remember that people above you are often eager for "news," especially good news, from the people like you who are on the front lines.

Q: "What if I run into an executive and he asks me, 'What's going on in your area?'"

A: Always have a Success Story to tell about yourself or your team. See Chapter 11 for how to create Success Stories.

Q: "I'm new. I don't know anybody. Where should I start?"

A: Take a tip from Susan, who says, "When I joined the company, I made up my own orientation program. Every day in the cafeteria, I found someone sitting alone and asked, 'May I join you?' then I asked 'What do you do here?' I was in charge of library and information services, and, in order to serve the organization well, I decided I needed to know a key person in each department. Every time I hire people I tell them, 'Your job is to represent the library, so get to know people.' I taught each of them my 'cafeteria method.' Now, I tell each of the 26 people I supervise to develop their own contact circle, 'Your group will be different from mine, and that way we'll know what the people we serve need—sometimes even before they know they need it.' Networking internally helps us form cross-functional teams and gather the intelligence that makes our department a catalyst for change."

Bonus: After Organizational Earthquakes, Rebuild Your Network

Reorganizations, mergers, acquisitions, and layoffs can destroy the relationships you've carefully built within your organization. You may feel like hunkering down and hiding. Don't! Reconstruct your network, using these ideas:

▶ Acknowledge that "the good old days" are gone forever, then—quickly—commit yourself wholeheartedly to the new enterprise.

▶ Focus up. Let your boss know you are ready to help to create the new order.

▶ Bring your subordinates on board. Meet one-on-one for lunch. Or get together after work. Create a new sense of camaraderie and adventure. Recommit to doing a good job. Look forward, not backward.

▶ Reach out to peers you relate with on the job—anyone whose job intersects yours.

▶ Escape your cubicle and build new bridges with related departments, functions, and divisions.

▶ Volunteer for cross-departmental teams and activities.

▶ Spend time shoring up relationships with customers, clients, suppliers, and vendors. (If they believe your company is in chaos, they may defect. Be positive. Also remember, these networking contacts could provide your next job.)

▶ Find ways to relate to competitors, perhaps through industry associations. Always be upbeat and positive about what's been going on in your organization. Boost your company's reputation, every chance you get. Remember, your next job could come from your current competitor.

CHAPTER 15

Make It Rain Clients

If you're a lawyer, CPA, or doctor, what's the word that's most abhorrent to you? How about "sales?" When you hear it, do you grimace? Flinch? Cringe? Blanch? The word "marketing" is only slightly less upsetting. So, you call it something else—"rainmaking."

Whatever you call it, you probably know that, in today's marketplace, even professionals like you have to sell. You must bring clients in the door, or you will find yourself on the way out!

"But," you plead, "Isn't there a *professional* way to do it?"

Law firms need "finders, minders, and grinders." Minders are people who handle clients; grinders grind out the work; and finders are rainmakers. All three are valuable, but in most firms everyone must market.

People who take active roles in professional associations find that they are a comfortable place to sell. The loss in billable hours is more than offset by these benefits: credibility for their firms; visibility that enhances their firms' reputations; referrals from other professionals; access to key people in business, government, and legal circles; and, of course, rainmaking.

You can come up with other comfortable ways to sell. Successful rainmakers know how to create networks from which referrals flow. In this chapter, you'll find out what people in professional services *really* think about networking. You'll discover new ways to develop your practice. You'll learn how to strategize and set up a professional Relationship Management Program for your firm. And you'll get advice on how to create the most powerful networking process of all—the Constellation.

177

What People Think

In a group of CPAs that included twenty-five-year veterans as well as those new to the profession, people voiced these concerns about networking:

▶ "I have so little free time I'm reluctant to spend it doing something I dislike. How can I get over my reluctance and fit networking into my already-too-busy life?"

▶ "Don't you have to spend a lot of time at this before you get any rewards?"

▶ "Do I begin talking about business or do I try small talk first?"

▶ "I tend to seek out people I know rather than new faces. How can I find ways to split my time and meet new people?"

▶ "Not only do I want to remember other people's names, I also want them to remember mine. How can I make that happen?"

▶ "How subtle or direct should I be about marketing my services when I meet someone for the first time?"

▶ "How do I get to the point of making reciprocal referrals?"

▶ "Can I afford to go to networking events or will I miss too much billable time?"

▶ "How can I follow up to develop my practice?"

▶ "How can I tactfully use social and business occasions to 'sell' my services?"

▶ "How can I find the 'movers and shakers' at a meeting?"

Most of these concerns aren't unique to professionals like you. But there are three things that make networking especially hard for you: your lack of time, your ambivalence about accepting client development as part of your role, and your conviction that you shouldn't have to sell yourself. Here's how to streamline the process and get more comfortable at it.

Professionalize Your Practice Development

Take a strategic view. Set up a Relationship Management Program to provide a structured, customized blueprint for your activities. Almost anyone can initiate this planning session. The benefits of careful planning include:

▶ Constant referrals to qualified clients

▶ Additional business from current clients

▶ Access to inside information on business trends and resources

▶ Higher visibility in your field and in the community

To make networking part of your overall business plan, assess and target, initiate and connect, track and measure, and renew and reassess.

Assess and target. Where have your current clients come from? Assess your current client base to determine how you found each other. Is there a pattern you can build on? Where are your potential clients? Which organizations and circles of influence will logically be your best targets?

Kent's architecture firm specializes in designing schools. He and his partners, therefore, should focus their networking efforts on organizations that serve school administrators. Although it makes sense to use this tactic, the number of businesspeople who actually seek out and become active in organizations that serve their clients is surprisingly small. Put your energy where your potential clients are.

Which organizations are members of your firm currently affiliated with? Can they justify their memberships or did they just join without thinking about who they need to meet? Can they explain exactly how those memberships put them in touch with the right people? How much time are they spending each month? What is the cost of belonging to each organization? Can they document the return on their investment? Use the chart in Chapter 5 to assess various Arenas.

Does it make more sense to target individuals rather than join

> You can do more than hope that your networking efforts will pay off. You can make it happen.

groups? If so, which individuals would provide the largest numbers of solid leads and referrals? How can you find these people?

What amount of time can and should people be spending on client development? If the primary goal is billable hours, how can the firm encourage and reward people for taking the time to develop networking relationships?

Initiate and connect. Once you have determined your targets and identified organizations and circles that you should be more active in, how are you going to deploy the members of your firm?

Pair up organizations and colleagues whose backgrounds or interests match. Set goals for the next six months and create networking Projects to achieve them. Use ideas in this book to get up to speed quickly and to become active and visible.

Track and measure. Devise a system for tracking leads and quantifying your efforts. Marshall was surprised to discover that twelve of fifteen new clients for his advertising firm came from one client services team. What were they doing? They had adopted a structured, pre-planned method for always asking for referrals.

Renew and reassess. Determine how you will stay in touch with prospects, referral sources, and past clients. How will you update them on new services and remind them of your expertise? What contact management system will you use? How long will you stay active in an organization if you are not getting any referrals through your contacts there?

Consider these questions as you plan:

1. What strategic goals and plans in our organization make Relationship Management a priority now?

2. Which relationships have brought us the best information and referrals in the past? What has been the pattern of development in those relationships?

3. What kinds of relationships do we need to stay informed in our field today? Who do we already know? Who do we need to know? Where will we meet these people?

4. What contacts do we already have who can provide introductions that will establish maximum credibility?

5. What behaviors tend to build trust with key contacts? What is the best protocol for initiating relationships? How can we best exhibit our Competence and Character to contacts?

6. What skills do we need to cultivate business connections? How are we going to train people over time? Do we need a formal training program to help people recognize the many ChoicePoints in their networking activities? Should we establish a mentoring program?

7. What do people have to offer individually, as they establish mutually beneficial business connections? Is each individual prepared to "sell" his or her own specialty and to explain why that service is superior?

8. Are people prepared to "cross sell," to pass prospects and referrals to others in the firm? What process do we have or could we develop to keep people informed about each other's areas of expertise?

9. What are the plans of each individual in our organization for making contacts in a variety of Arenas?

10. What systems are in place to support members of our firm as they go forward? Are there ways to reward people for their efforts? Are we sending a conflicting message when we emphasize billable hours and also encourage networking?

Make Conversations Count

Here are some tips to help you get the most from your networking activities.

▶Often, people ask questions of professionals at networking events that are requests for professional guidance. These folks may not mean to ask for a free consultation; they may just be trying to make conversation with you on a topic you might find interesting. You'll want to develop a clear, but clever way to encourage your conversation partner to make an appointment.

▶Work on your answer to the question, "What do you do?" When you reply with your profession ("I'm an attorney"), you make your conversation partner do all the work. Instead, come up with a BEST/TEST answer (see Chapter 9) that gets the conversation going. Rose doesn't even mention that she's a CPA in her answer. She says, "We work with passionate entrepreneurs, helping them grow their businesses." Or, "We help people increase their net worth. We showed a client that formed as an LLC how they are overpaying their income tax." Be sure your example highlights a part of your practice that you want to expand and not something you are lukewarm about doing.

> **Networking can help you turn contacts into clients.**

▶To let people know about your specialty, have interesting information that you are comfortable giving away. Eldon works with businesspeople when they want to move from sole proprietorships to corporations. He has amassed a lot of useful information for business owners who are feeling overwhelmed as their businesses expand overnight, and often suggests that they join an executive roundtable group, so they can get advice from other entrepreneurs.

▶Listen with an ear for problems. When Conrad mentioned his father's illness, Kira introduced him to a counselor who dealt with succession planning for family businesses. The counselor later sent the family back to Kira, who handled the legal issues.

▶Don't define your role too narrowly. Marcie used to say, "I am a business analyst and management consultant, who specializes in setting up flex-time programs." She realized that potential clients often didn't appreciate how much impact flex-time programs could have on employee turnover. So, now she says, "I help companies retain employees." She finds that talking about the problem, rather than the solution brings her more opportunities.

▶Tell Success Stories. (See Chapter 11.) One way to memorably describe your problem-solving capabilities is to tell stories. Respecting client confidentiality, you can disguise the particulars and tell how you solved a problem, or saved someone money, or increased productivity or profits. Make your stories brief and dynamic.

When someone asked Mark, a CPA, "What's new?" he said, "I just saved a client, whose business almost tanked last year, a ton of money by convincing him to move from his rented office back home."

What's One Conversation Worth?

Often, people who market their services can determine the value of a single conversation. Joyce, a financial consultant, met a man who asked her, "What would you do if you had $600,000 to invest?" Her answer obviously impressed him because he did ask her to manage his portfolio. She figures she made $18,000 from that one conversation.

When Chuck, who teaches problem-solving in corporations, took his seat on an airplane, he was delighted to find himself next to a person who had just been promoted to head up the creativity department at a large chemical company. Unfortunately, that man was exhausted, and Chuck was able to have only a short conversation with him before the man fell asleep and slept through the entire flight. However, as Chuck boarded the rental car van, another man caught up with him. "Excuse me for eavesdropping," he said, "but I was sitting behind you and I'm very interested in the kind of creativity training you were talking about." Chuck has provided $48,000 worth of seminars for that roundabout contact.

Create Constellations

Your strongest referrals can come from other professionals with whom you share clients. Put together your own referral group— your Constellation—by forming alliances with top-notch professionals in other fields who have access to your market. One group is made up of a lawyer, a CPA, an interior designer who concentrates on the senior citizen market, and a person who runs estate sales. When a widow decides to move into a retirement apartment, the estate sale person can refer her to the interior designer. Either the estate sale person or the interior designer can refer her to the CPA, who can refer her to the lawyer. The referral cycle can begin with any member of the group so that a client for one of the members soon becomes a client for all of the members. (See Chapter 16 for more on creating a Constellation and Chapter 18 for more on referral groups.)

George, a Chicago CPA, has been developing Constellations for many years. "The key to business is obtaining new clients," he says. "The problem is to do it professionally. Networking is the solution."

As he helps other professionals grow their practices, he reaps the benefits. He cultivates relationships with bankers, lawyers, insurance agents, and stockbrokers—all people who can refer business his way. "Once I have identified potential candidates to link up with, allocating the time to get to know them is the biggest challenge." He goes at it systematically, setting up a series of meetings. He meets with people over lunch or dinner, visits them in their offices, and invites them to his. "I don't go and say, 'I need you to give me new business.' I say 'Here's what I can do for you and, hopefully, you'll be in position to pay back the favor.'

> Create customer-common alliances with other business people. Refer your customers to your allies, and get referrals in return.

"I do a selling job on myself and a fact-finding job on the other person," he says. He finds out exactly what the person does so he can qualify contacts for him and refer the right clients. "I make sure if a contact needs a banker, I send him to the right one. You need to know specialists in various areas, but I cultivate only a handful of 'partners.' I want to keep them happy. I couldn't keep eighteen bankers happy."

Actually, George doesn't *send* any clients to his 'partners.' His trademark is that he *hand-delivers* the clients. He calls the banker, makes an appointment, and personally takes his client to the banker's office.

He's trained all seventy-five professionals in his firm to use the same practice development method. When he recruits on campuses for new accountants, he makes sure they are marketing-oriented. As new grads join the firm, George trains them to build relationships with people in their own age bracket, creating networks that will grow in influence and power through the years as their careers advance.

Cross-Sell Your Clients

Can you sell more services to existing clients? The cost of getting new business far exceeds the cost of getting more business from clients you already serve. That's why internal referrals are so important in professional services firms.

Conrad, a CPA, teaches the client services teams in his firm to handle their engagements so that they listen for other organizational problems his firm might help to solve. His teams are trained to pick up on any needs they hear about. "You say the staff needs training on this new accounting software? Our training department can do that for you. I'll set up a meeting." "You say the CEO is having a business planning retreat for all the top staff? Our management consultants can facilitate your strategic planning session. Let me call Kathryn, and we'll get our people ready to make a proposal to your CEO." Conrad's people cross-sell the firm's capabilities constantly.

Make Asking for Referrals a Ritual

If you don't get referrals, perhaps you haven't established a routine for asking for them. Make asking an integral part of what you do with every client. You'd never fail to mention billing procedures, would you? Asking for referrals should be even more central.

Bill Cates, dubbed the "Champion of Referral Selling," suggests "foreshadowing" as a way to let the client know that you'll eventually ask. Early in the relationship, often even before someone has become a client, it's possible to "foreshadow" with comments like, "Since my business is built on referrals . . ." or "Sam was referred to me by Janna at Kidder, Wilson, and Smith."

Teach everyone in your firm the following eight steps so that they know how to ask clients or their business contacts for referrals.

1. *Recall your track record.* Encourage your client or contact to remember what you did for him. Ask, "What do you particularly appreciate about the way we worked with you, handled your project, managed your engagement, pursued your case?"

2. *Remind clients that you count on referrals.* Encourage clients to become part of your referral system. Say, "You probably remember my saying that about 60 percent of our business comes from referrals from satisfied clients like you."

3. *Review their circles.* Help clients or contacts think of people who might be ready for your services. Say, "I know you're on the

board of the Country Club. Are there others on the board who are also ready to do some serious financial planning?" Or, "I was so pleased when you said your partners complimented you about the new addition we designed for your house. Are any of them ready to look at some photos of other work we've done, and talk with me about what they'd like to do to update their homes?" Or, "Which new members of the Chamber of Commerce do you recommend I contact to let them know about our firm's accounting services?"

4. *Receive specifics.* Ask for any specific information that will help make your first contact successful. "Let me be sure I've got Lisa's last name spelled correctly. Does she have a cell phone?" "What is a good time to reach Paul? At home or at work?" "Which of our services do you think Martina would find most interesting right now?" "Why do you think Ron would be interested at this time?"

5. *Raise the possibility of success.* Encourage clients and contacts to pave the way. Say, "It would be really helpful to me if you'd give Mary a call to let her know I'll be getting in touch. Naturally, I'd appreciate your telling her how satisfied you were with my work." Or, "Would you be willing to send Sacha a note telling her I'm going to call?" Or, "How about if the three of us get together for breakfast Friday? That way you can introduce us, and Fred can hear firsthand about what we've done for you."

6. *Rapidly make contact.* If your client gives you a referral, follow up quickly. If you don't, it could be embarrassing to you and your client.

7. *Recount the results.* Get back to your client with your thanks. Give appreciation, whether the contact resulted in business or not. Closing the loop and letting your client know what happened is just common courtesy. In some types of referral relationships, you may have agreed to pay a referral fee—a percentage of the dollar amount of the business. If you made that kind of agreement, be sure the check goes out quickly.

8. *Reciprocate.* Return the favor. Be on the lookout for ways you can help your client succeed. Provide resources, information, or referrals to the client or contact who gave you the referral.

Go ahead, make it rain.

CHAPTER 16

(Net)Work from Home

Are you part of the home-based business revolution—the growing segment of the working population attracted by the 30-second commute, the flexible hours, the tax breaks, the idea of being your own boss, and a sky's-the-limit income potential? The *Wall Street Journal* reports that there are now 30 million home-based businesses, and that 8,000 new ones are starting up each week.

Tune In to the Trends

Three trends are responsible for the surge in stay-at-home workers. First, mergers and corporate downsizing continue to "free up the futures" of many talented, experienced people. Second, technologies necessary to set up an office at home are widely available, relatively inexpensive, getting easier for people to use. Third, the "sandwich generation" has a need for more flexible schedules as they juggle child care and elder care.

According to *Success Magazine*, the top ten home-based businesses include business consulting and services, computer services and programming, financial consulting and services, marketing, advertising and public relations, medical practices and services, graphics and visual arts, security, real estate, writing, and independent sales. And, of course, there are many franchises that work well as home-based businesses, such as Computer Tots, Decorating Den, and Molly Maids. Some types of franchises start off as home-based businesses, then later experience such growth that they move to commercial space.

Conquer the Challenges

Two challenges arise for people who are (net)working from home.

If you're someone who thrived on the camaraderie of belonging to a large organization and having lots of coworkers to kibitz with, working solo may seem lonely. You may spend too much time attending events to get the contact you crave. If that's you, make a plan for your networking activity. Make good decisions about which events and which groups will give you the best returns. Plan your calendar accordingly.

On the other hand, if you like working alone, you might get too comfortable "cocooning." Do you hate to put on that suit and head out to the luncheon meeting? Are you too busy to volunteer for the hospital fundraiser? Are you so tied to your terminal that you're reluctant to meet new people and to reconnect with people you know? Don't forget that business success depends on networking for new clients or customers and on gathering the latest business intelligence so you stay at the cutting edge.

Do you have a goal that is attainable through networking? Review Chapter 5. Decide why you are networking. Create your Project. Then, finding the time to network will make sense. Schedule your networking just like you schedule your other business activities. Use every social and business event as a time to explore trends that will affect your business (that new zoning law), find resources (that space to hold client focus group meetings), and tell people about your successes (that appointment to the governor's small business advisory committee). Proactively look for and give leads and referrals.

Successful home-based businesspeople use networking to find customers, suppliers, distributors, lenders, investors, joint-venture partners, other kinds of partners, and mentors. In the process, you will strike up valuable connections that will fuel your business growth for years to come.

When Jeff wanted to explore the idea of franchising his business, he thought of Al, a lawyer he had grown to trust and respect as he worked on committees at the Board of Trade. From her contacts at the Northern Virginia Technology Council, Sau Ching learned how to prepare a package to send to potential investors when she was ready to expand her business importing dolls. She might have followed guidelines in a book or from an Internet article, but her chance to talk over the fine points with other businesspeople who'd been through the venture capital process saved her precious time and ensured her success.

Many entrepreneurs find themselves networking as they go about their day-to-day tasks. Think of how often you reach out to shake hands and say hello. Now, think of what would happen if a good percentage of those encounters generated sales leads or productive new ideas. Sound far-fetched? It shouldn't—not if you're as prepared to take advantage of chance meetings as you are of regular business appointments.

> **People want to do business with people they trust.**

Lee's business was making costumes. She needed a source for unusual trimmings. She found one, sitting next to her on a flight to Louisville.

Remember, you're not networking until the people you meet know your name, understand what type of customers or clients you want, trust your Character and Competence, and believe you'll reward them for their efforts on your behalf.

In this chapter, you'll find tips for making networking from home work for you. Do refer to other chapters for additional ideas before you finalize your networking business plan.

Link Up Your Life and Your Livelihood

Make linking your life. Instead of thinking of networking as something else to put on your already crowded to-do list, see it as life itself. Everywhere you go, from back-yard barbecues to trade shows, you meet people. Be sure that you can answer the questions, "What do you do?" and "What's new?" in ways that teach people about your service or product. Be prepared with up-to-date examples of your recent successes, projects, and clients. The more you tell, the more you sell.

Linda owns Bed and Biscuit, an inn for pets. She always has a new story that reminds people of the tender loving care she lavishes on her animal guests. "I'm boarding a llama this week," she reports, "and she's so happy when I groom her that she stands very still and breathes loudly through her nose." Or, "Mattie, the German

Shepherd, had puppies with me while her owners were on vacation. They were so happy with our newborn care that they mentioned us in their Christmas letter!"

Join—or start—a referral group. A referral group or Constellation can bring you plenty of business. Follow the guidelines in the Bonus at the end of this chapter. Emily, of Discovery Toys, started her own group of six women who all live in her neighborhood. The strength of their group is its diversity. In addition to Emily, the group includes a musician who plays for private parties, a graphic artist, a nanny-finder, an image consultant, and an interior designer. They used each other's services and bought each other's products to get acquainted. The classical guitarist had a session with the image consultant and came up with a new look that got her noticed and added flair to her performance. The nanny-finder hosted a party for all her nannies at which Emily showed her toys.

Create customer-common Constellations.

Bart, an insurance agent, teamed up with an attorney and a financial advisor. Reva, owner of Hire a Handywoman, a home fix-it service, belongs to a group that has thirty-eight members, all in different businesses. She can track 20 percent of her income to that group—during her first year of membership.

Spiff up your image. Act and appear in public as if you had an office downtown in the high rent district. Remember, you may meet people at the grocery store or library or copy center. So, wear business dress or at least business casual when you go out, not your oldest, grubbiest sweat suit—even if that's your favorite work outfit! Always have your business cards with you, even on a run to the post office.

Angie was in line at the post office waiting to charge up her postage meter when she ran into Loren, an independent sales rep doing the same errand. He sells women's handbags; Angie markets a local craftsman's line of purses and briefcases. A year later, they still laugh about how they met when Loren commented on her leather backpack. Loren now sells Angie's line.

Choose to stand out. Select three to six Arenas and become visible in them. Pick one, such as a local home-based business association, for the business support you need from peers. Choose two populated by your clients or by people who can refer work to you. Susan, a caterer, became active in The Association of Wedding Professionals. Jaime, a remodeler, joined a real estate group, figuring those people might provide some good referrals to home-owners who needed to have a few things done before putting their houses on the market. Use your hobbies or interests to make contact. Evan, a computer consultant, counts seven new clients this year from contacts he made at his health club. Keep your family up-to-date about exactly what you are doing and what kinds of resources or clients you want to find.

Make sure people hear about you before they hear from you. Imagine meeting a prospect at a networking event who says, "Didn't I see an article by you in last month's

Make sure people hear about you before they hear from you.

Chamber newsletter?" Or, "I heard you interviewed on the Women's Resource Network radio show several weeks ago." Getting visible in organizations and in your community allows you to make a name for yourself and enhance your credibility with people who count—even before you meet.

Pick your not-so-prime-times to network. Everybody's got high and low energy times and busy and not so busy times. Go with the flow. Mari's mornings are hectic, so she avoids breakfast meetings. Don is a morning person so he schedules meetings early in the day. Many home-based business people comment that they shy away from lunch events which can eat up three or even four hours in the middle of the day. Analyze your biorhythms, your work flow, and your family obligations and plan accordingly.

Accomplish your Agenda. Decide before you leave the house what you want to accomplish. Create your Agenda every day and focus on it. Here are some sample Agenda items:

▶ "Meet at least two people on the Board of Directors and offer to be on a committee to raise my visibility in the organization."

▶ "Find out which temporary help agency others have used and liked."

▶ "Meet a divorce lawyer who might eventually send tax work my way."

▶ "Identify businesses large enough to hold catered events several times a year and invite them to my Tasting Party."

▶ "Meet people whose parents are considering moving into a retirement complex."

Reconnect and Follow Through. When you return to your office from a networking event, go through any business cards you received and decide how to reconnect. Do this immediately, before you get caught up in the tasks on your desk. Ideally, you'll use one of the many contact management software packages on the market to keep track of people and stay in touch. In addition to putting phone numbers and addresses at your fingertips, your system will also alert you to Follow Through (e.g., "Call Fred March 1 about the annual dinner") and will make creating mailing labels a cinch.

Promote your business creatively. Since you don't have a store front and don't have a big sign, what can you do to draw attention to your business? Gina, a watercolorist, teamed up with Gary, who owns a frame shop in a busy mall. They hosted a Saturday "sidewalk art show" to display his frames and her paintings. Candy's stuffed animal business, Bunny Rabbit Babies, hopped in the spring time, but hibernated in the fall and winter. She donated fifteen bunnies to the playroom in the children's wing of the hospital, which led to a contract with the hospital gift shop. That exposure led to another contract with a hotel gift shop. Those two contracts tripled her business in one year.

Holler "Help!"—and get it. With only the cat and the philodendron to talk to, you may feel you are home alone. The truth is that, all across town, others just like you are wondering, "Am I on the right track?" "Do I have what it takes?" "How can I grow my business?" "Who can I talk to when I get down in the dumps?" The two best sources of support are other home-based business people like yourself and hired experts.

Get the support and encouragement you need by networking with others who work from home. Lynnette, who is in business for herself and by herself, already belonged to several networking groups of people who do training and development. But she wanted to talk over her business strategy and get support from people who were outside her own profession. So, she and three other entrepreneurs started The Presidents' Group. They meet once a month for an hour or so in a restaurant. First, each person has a fifteen-minute turn. Everybody gets a chance to tell about a recent accomplishment. For people who work alone, celebrating success with others is important. "At first, we were shy about sharing our accomplishments. I guess we all grew up being told not to brag," Lynnette says. "But we found that when we took credit for our successes, it was easier to tackle the problems." Next, people take turns asking for help or feedback from the group on one issue or challenge. This problem can be anything from "How can I market my services so that I have more work in December?" to "How do you like this design for my new business card?" In the group, Lynnette says, "The friendships deepened as our business savvy increased." Four years later, the group is still meeting.

Use your network to hire experts. Ask around for an accountant who specializes in home-based businesses, or for a graphic artist who can give you the look you want in your next brochure. You can't do it all yourself. Often, those professionals you hire will turn out to be some of your best referral sources. After all, they know exactly what you do. And they know that, when your business grows, so will theirs.

Bonus: Create a Constellation

Some of the most mutually beneficial contacts are the people who share customers. Put together your own group—a Constellation of people who have customers in common with you. Form alliances with top-notch professionals in other fields who have access to your market. For example, a financial advisor invited an insurance broker, a realtor, a CPA, and a lawyer to be part of her group. A client for one of the members often becomes a client for all of the members.

Here's how to start your Constellation:

▶Notice what other businesses your clients use most often.

▶Identify five or six potential partners.

▶Spend time with them individually. Teach your Character and Competence and learn about theirs. You must be able to trust that they will treat your valuable clients well before you invite them to join your Constellation.

▶Find out exactly what your potential partners do so you can qualify clients for them and refer the right ones to them. Teach them exactly what kinds of clients you are looking for, so they can do the same for you.

▶Whenever possible, plan a face-to-face meeting to introduce your Constellation member to the client you're referring. When that's not possible, do all you can to warm up your colleague's first call to the client.

▶Meet regularly so that you can keep up-to-date on new services and new successes. A fourth Friday lunch works well for many groups.

Sandra, a marketing consultant, created The Marketing Consortium. "Think of it as a six-leaf clover," she suggests, "with me in the middle and six related companies on the leaves." These companies do media buying, sales promotions, direct marketing, sales training, new business development, and strategic planning. Sandra's company provides creative support with ads and brochures. She always asks her clients if they need anything her "leaves" could provide. "I don't get a percentage; I just expect business in return."

Constellations are one very targeted way to create your network. You don't need to know lots of people; you need to know the right people well.

CHAPTER 17

Make the Most of Your Memberships

There are two ways to create your network: link up with people individually and join organizations. Some of your best networking contacts will come from one-on-one relationships—your next door neighbor, your accountant, your cousin in Tulsa. You find these people, or they find you, outside any formal organization. You'll also benefit from becoming involved with several groups if you select them carefully, keeping in mind the time and money you have to spend and your career and business goals.

Size Your Network to Fit Your Needs

There is no magic number for the size of your network. If fifty people think of you when a certain kind of expertise is needed, speak well of you to their colleagues, and consider you a source of advice and information, you may have an excellent network—depending on your current situation and goals.

If, however, you fear being laid off, want to start your own business someday, have a business that could profit from having more customers or clients, or are facing a major life change (such as moving across the country, or leaving the military), then you need to think bigger.

We recommend that you become active in six networking Arenas. That may sound like a lot, but consider that you are probably already a member of a family, a religious organization, a professional or trade group, a leisure-time activity (hobby group, health club, etc), and you may have "kid" connections. Those groups add up to five Arenas. Think of all of those venues as networking opportunities.

Link Up One-on-One

Your personal network will include people from many different sources. You may forge strong business alliances with:

▶ Coworkers, past and current.

▶ Bosses, past and current.

▶ Neighbors.

▶ Past college professors or continuing education instructors.

▶ Relatives.

▶ People who provide services to you (your doctor, dentist, office supply store proprietor, etc.).

Customize your one-on-one network by being on the lookout for chance encounters. See every accidental meeting as an opportunity to explore new ideas, find out about new marketplaces, or just enjoy the serendipitous connections that life sends your way.

Rita, a CPA, stops every morning for coffee. She made it a point to learn the names of the people who serve her and chat about work—theirs and hers. One day, as she was waiting in line, the clerk asked the customer in front of her, "How are you doing today?" The man said, "Terrible! I've got to find a new accountant. Mine moved to Chicago." The clerk pointed at Rita and said, "There's one right behind you! Rita, meet Alonzo."

Access Anybody

Regardless of whoever you need to know, somebody you know most likely knows somebody who knows them. This small-world phenomenon was studied in-depth by the late Stanley Milgram, a psychologist. What he discovered proves that it's possible for you to make contact with just about anyone you wish—because you have friends who have friends who have friends.

Milgram wondered if it would be possible for a package to be passed from a specific, randomly selected person in Omaha to a specific, randomly selected person in Boston using "friends" (people you know by their first names) as the conduits. He discovered that not only was it possible, but it took surprisingly few people—typically only five or six—for two individuals half a continent apart to make contact through a chain of acquaintances.

As Milgram explained it, if you know just fifty people on a first-name basis, and they know fifty people, you have access to 2,500 contacts. If that group each knows fifty people, you could potentially reach 125,000 people. And if they each know fifty people you could reach more than six million contacts.

When Annette, who lives in Kansas City, was attending the international conference of her professional association in Montreal, she went to a reception honoring international delegates. In the corner of the room sat a woman wearing a sari. Because her sister Maureen, who lives in Washington, D.C., had just adopted a baby from India, Annette went over and introduced herself. She said, "I have a new nephew who was born in India. "The woman introduced herself, saying, "I'm Cerena from Bombay." Amazingly, Cerena's mother had been Annette's new nephew's foster mother in India.

You may hear people talk about various networking "generations." Your "first generation" network includes the people you know directly. Your "second generation" network includes the people known by the people you know. The "third generation" includes their contacts. And the "fourth generation"—the six-plus million pool—includes their contacts. It is possible to relate to "fourth generation" contacts, but only if you've been passed along by people who have established a great deal of trust.

Michael, who works for a social justice non-profit organization, points out the importance of asking people you know for the resources you need. "What I need is often two or three links down the chain. So I put out the word. Networking at the beginning of the project for almost any initiative I put together is one way to insure that it will turn out to be effective with our constituents."

Of course, the range and quality of your contacts will dramatically affect your ability to use the small-world phenomenon to find resources and opportunities. Great networkers know people who know people who know people in a variety of Arenas—organizations, subcultures, marketplaces, groups, and niches.

Take MaryLou in Philadelphia, for instance. Her new boss Shelia moved to town from Seattle. Shelia's hobby is collecting antique inkwells. "How obscure," thinks MaryLou, who knows nothing about inkwells or antiques. But, using her network, she discovers that a friend of a friend is immersed in the antique subculture of Pennsylvania. MaryLou is able to connect Shelia with the people who know the best shows, the best appraisers, and the best dealers in Pennsylvania. Shelia is thrilled and sees that MaryLou is resourceful and creative.

The possibilities are limitless. But your time and money are not. So that's why great networkers don't just count on one-on-one connections. They join groups to put them in contact with large numbers of people.

Join Groups

Joining organizations is the best way to build relationships with a multitude of people and expand your personal and professional network by creating instant Associates. For any given interest, job type, industry, or business, you'll have many possible groups to choose from.

Jon is an architect in Easton, Maryland. He specializes in designing hospitals and has a personal and professional interest in landscaping. He *could* join the American Institute of Architects, and any of its many special interest groups. He *could* join the Board of Trade, and the American Institute of Landscape Architects, and the local Rotary Club, and the American Association of Hospital Administrators, and the Chesapeake Healthcare Association. Then, there's the group that's restoring plant life along the Chesapeake Bay. Or how about the Lion's Club? Or he could join the alumni group for his alma mater, Boston University. Or how about a referral group? Jon has many ChoicePoints. You probably do too. Jon needs a process to narrow down the choices and find the best groups for him. So do you.

Choose Groups Strategically

Use the list that follows as you make strategic choices about which Settings to focus on. Not all groups are equally useful for networking. Your choice will depend on your goals and on the characteristics of the group.

These Arenas are arranged from the most highly structured and intentional networking groups at the top of the list, to the most "accidental" and serendipitous at the bottom. The groups at the top focus on bringing people together to do business; the groups farther down the list have other goals and networking becomes a sideline. Groups at the top will actually teach you how to network and outline appropriate behaviors. In groups farther down the list, the ground rules are foggier, so the more skilled at networking you are, the more successful you'll be.

Understand the Hierarchy

Customer Common Groups. These groups (Constellations) are made up of businesses that have customers in common. Owners of businesses that beautify and maintain the home, for example, an interior designer, a real estate agent, a home remodeler, a lawn care professional, and a chimney sweep might band together to refer work to each other. To start your own group, see the Bonus: Create a Constellation at the end of Chapter 16.

Special Purpose Networks. Some networks are created with one purpose in mind. In one Midwest city, for example, entrepreneurs started a special network to attract venture financing. Job hunting support groups are another example.

Business Referral Groups. Small or home-based business people, sales professionals, or people in professional services and others benefit from these groups. The groups' missions are tightly focused on getting business and generating referrals from each other. Only one business in each "category" may join. For example, members will include only one florist, one electrician, one accountant. At meetings, members learn about each other's products and services. A commitment to attend and generate leads is essential to the success of the group. See Chapter 18 for a detailed look at these groups.)

Networking Organizations. These groups often have the word "networking" in their names. They may have other goals, such as professional development for members. But they will focus on providing opportunities to build relationships. To help people get acquainted, these organizations may offer special interest groups, such as a book club, an investment group or a business owners group. One women's networking organization, The Central Exchange in Kansas City, has as its motto: "The thing that sets us apart is the people we bring together."

> **Make strategic choices about where to network.**

Professional and Trade Associations. Whatever your job type, whatever your industry or profession, there is at least one professional association for you, if not several. Ask experienced people in your chosen field to recommend which one would be right for you. Watch the business section of your newspaper for meeting announcements. Check the Encyclopedia of Associations at your local library, or go to a group's website for membership information and the name of a local contact.

Industry-Specific Organizations. These organizations put you in touch with people in other companies. An aviation association, for example, brings together people from all of the carriers, as well as related businesses. Because they face similar problems, these people can be great resources for each other. Visibility in one of these groups may help your upward mobility, since there is usually a lot of opportunity for job movement among similar organizations. Within these industry-specific groups, there often are subgroups for people with various kinds of jobs—a purchasing group, for example. These subgroups provide access to your peers and leaders across the industry.

Workplace Task Forces/Committees. Don't forget opportunities to network at work. Get out of your cubicle and mix with others by serving on the Run for Fun Committee, or The United Way planning team, or the Diversity Task Force. These are good ways to increase your visibility at work and to hear about other areas of your organization that might need your skills.

Chambers of Commerce. Whether you're self-employed or work for an organization, your local Chamber of Commerce will welcome you. Although this group's mission focuses on civic improvement, economic development, and legislative efforts to favor business, at Chamber meetings, you'll come in contact with people from a wide variety of workplaces with a wide variety of interests. Networking is certainly a big part of the picture.

Civic and Service Organizations. These groups include such organizations as Rotary International, the Lions Club, and many others. They focus on service to the community and civic improvement. The relaxed, informal conversations you have there help others trust you and, long-term, can lead to job opportunities, new customers, and access to all kinds of resources.

Volunteer Groups. When Simon agreed to help build new play equipment in the community park, little did he know hammering nails with Martin would lead to a five-year contract to videotape every corporate presentation made at Martin's company. Volunteering is a way to blend a passion for giving back to the community with the chance to establish long-term business relationships as you demonstrate your Character and Competence.

Hobby/Health/Sports Activities. Some of Pat's first customers when he started his home-based graphic design business were the people he'd met singing in a barbershop quartet. As you enjoy leisure-time activities, remember to teach others about your skills and talents and Listen Generously for how you can contribute to the quality of their personal and professional lives.

Sondra and Marilyn both showed up at the health club at 6 a.m. on Mondays, Wednesdays, and Fridays. They could have just continued to exchange pleasantries, but instead used their exercise time to explore ideas about "life after the corporation." Two years, and lots of miles on the treadmill later, they quit their jobs and started a painting and wallpapering business.

Alumni Groups. A special kind of camaraderie grows out of having attended the same school. Alumni clubs put you in touch with people of all ages and walks of life. Although these clubs focus on promoting the school, raising funds, or supporting the teams, networking is an important part of the mix.

Religious Organizations. While business may not be the first thing you talk about at your church, synagogue, or mosque, it's undeniably true that being active in a religious community does establish relationships from which businesses and careers may eventually grow. Bob and George got to know each other so well at choir practice, that when George was asked to open up a new division in Milwaukee, Bob introduced him to his brother there.

Kid Connections. Your son plays on a soccer team or a basketball team or takes swimming lessons. How many times have you waited impatiently for the coach to end practice when you could have been developing your relationships with other parents? Kudos go to Amy whose sidelines conversations with Amera resulted in Amy providing some management training for Amera's organization—even though their daughters were on rival teams!

Seatmates. There you are, in an airplane for three hours, elbow to elbow with your seatmate. Sure, you might want to read or nap, but remember that a lot of travelers make business contacts with people they meet on airplanes. On a trip to Chicago, Bob sat next to David, a sales rep for a box manufacturing company. Bob told David he was looking for a heart-shaped box for his company's new specialty food product. David sent him the specs the next day and got the contract.

Wild Cards. Networking with people whose perspective is completely different from yours broadens your horizon in unexpected ways. As you seek out contacts with people you seem to have nothing in common, each conversation becomes an adventure. Assume that everyone you meet is important. These wild card contacts can be winners.

Any place people are is a networking opportunity . . . if you have the know-how.

Know the Group Before You Join

To find the right networking groups, associations, or organizations for you, check the Internet, the phone book, your local library, or the business pages of your newspaper. Ask other people in your profession what organizations they benefit from the most. Ask customers and clients what groups they belong to. There may be an "associate member" category for suppliers to their industries.

Once you've identified a few organizations, remember that you are about to place a very talented person—you—in a key position, so look before you leap. Attend a couple of meetings as a guest. Talk to new members and board members. Read several issues of the newsletter. Scan the membership directory. Before you write your check and commit your time, assess the organization's value to you by answering the following questions:

1. How many members are there? The bigger the better for networking, but it may be easier to move into leadership positions or gain visibility in other ways in smaller groups.

2. Can I get excited about the group's mission? Will its activities help me reach my networking goals?

3. Are people in the group likely to need my product or service or to refer business to me? Are people in the group likely to provide valuable resources or information?

4. What do people say about the group? What's its reputation in the profession or community?

5. What opportunities will the group offer me to associate with my peers? With stars in the field?

6. Does the group set a good networking culture by encouraging people to introduce themselves and talk to each other about important business and career Agendas?

7. Does the group have special activities to help newcomers feel welcome and meet people?

8. How easy is it to participate? How quickly could I move into a leadership role that would give me visibility and career experience?

9. Do the leaders seem genuinely excited about their participation or are they playing the "somebody has to do it" game?

10. Are the programs cutting edge? Do the topics and speakers provide valuable professional growth?

11. What would my time commitment be? Can I make that commitment for at least one year?

12. What exactly could I contribute to this group in order to become visible?

Orchestrate Who Knows You

Joining a group doesn't mean you join anybody's network—or that they join yours. Your membership gives you a place to develop relationships with your fellow members, who are your Associates. Great networkers work on becoming visible and valuable, and as a consequence, memorable. Sure, what you know is important. And who you know is important. But focus your energy on expanding the number of people who know YOU.

Use the organizations you join to:

▶Demonstrate your skills and expertise.

▶Discover new career directions or make a job change.

▶Gain recognition for your accomplishments and successes.

▶Find new resources and best practices.

▶Establish your reputation with people you might want to network with.

Take a high-profile role in organizations you belong to. Write an article for the newsletter. Provide a program. Staff the registration table at the monthly meeting. Get elected to the board of directors. Set up a job bank if your group doesn't have one. Enter your work in the annual awards program—an excellent way to become known for your abilities. Demonstrate your speaking skills, your budgetary wizardry, your organizing expertise, your leadership prowess.

When people see you in action in an organization, they make up their minds about your Character and Competence—even if they've never met you. If you do a great job as treasurer, people will assume that you are an excellent IT manager or an outstanding salesperson. Conversely, if you've promised to do something, but don't come through, people will assume that you are not a competent attorney or public relations practitioner. It's the All or Nothing Rule: If you do one thing well, people will assume you do everything well.

The strength and expanse of your network depends on how many people know you so well that when resources or opportunities drop into their lives, you pop into their minds as the person to call.

The Twelve Biggest Mistakes Members Make

1. They join, but don't go. They show up so sporadically that they can't reap the many benefits of membership.

2. They appear, but don't interact. They eat another olive, listen to the speaker, and leave.

3. They skip the networking portion, arriving just in time for the meal. They duck out just as the speaker finishes. Then they wonder why networking doesn't work for them.

4. They talk and sit with people they already know.

5. They make no effort to be visible; instead, they try to blend into the crowd.

6. They wait for others to make the first moves.

7. They think handing out business cards is networking.

8. They give up too soon. They hop from one organization to another, never giving themselves or others time to establish relationships.

9. They have "non-conversations." ("Hi, how are you?" "Not bad. How are you?" "Not bad. What's new?") They never get around to productive conversations.

10. They arrive without an Agenda. They come without any idea of what they have To Give or what they want To Get.

11. They are unaware of "netiquette" within the group. They violate "good networking" protocols.

12. They forget that the best way to show Character and Competence is to contribute time and energy.

Jump Right In

You don't have to wait to be elected to the board. You don't even have to sign up with a committee. Here are ten ways to jumpstart your participation in any group and to instantly begin to get involved.

1. *Come with a purpose.* More than 85 percent of people we surveyed confessed that, when they attend networking events, they have no specific purpose in mind, nothing they want to find or connect with, or learn. Before you go, decide what you want To Get—and what you have To Give. See Chapter 10 for step-by-step instructions on setting your Agenda.

2. *Plan ahead.* What can you do before a networking event to make sure you meet the people you need to meet? Call the administrator and ask for a list of attendees, so you know who is coming, or go to the group's website. You may find photos of board members, or a list of people who have won awards, or mini-profiles of members. This information can be used as conversation starters.

3. *Show up.* Arrive early and stay late. Be in the moment. Clear your mind. Set aside thoughts of work piling up back at the office. Give quality time to your contacts.

> After you become a member, the important work of creating relationship begins.

4. *Act like a host, not a guest.* You are president of your own network, even when you are attending an organization's event! Take responsibility for the success of the meeting. Greet newcomers, even if you aren't yet an old-hand yourself. As you make others comfortable, you'll feel more comfortable too.

5. *Give yourself a job.* Look around and find a way to be helpful. Pitch in at the registration desk. Pass out programs. Doing something will give you a reason for starting conversations.

6. *Introduce yourself to the leaders.* Seek out the president, membership chair, or program chair. Ask questions about the organization. Tell them why you have joined or are thinking about joining.

7. *Talk and sit with people you don't know.* Nearly 75 percent of people we surveyed admitted that they end up sitting next to the people they came with. If you are going to the event with people from your own office, agree beforehand that you won't sit together.

8. *Link up with your competitors.* Often people avoid talking with people who are in the same business or profession. But they can be excellent contacts, and may even refer business to you, eventually. Be ready to offer some information or a resource to your competitor to start a positive interaction.

9. *Help others connect.* Introduce people to each other and build your reputation as an expert networker. Say, "Oh, Sarah—I just met Ona, who has also just started her own business. Let me introduce you to her."

10. *Show off your wares or your services.* Provide a demonstration or a sample. Contribute a door prize. Do a display. Speak on a panel. Gayle, who sells fine leather products, carries a briefcase that shows off her wares.

CHAPTER 18

Rev Up Referral Groups

What if, all over town, there were people who knew your business so well and who were so invested in your success that they consistently referred just the right kind of clients and resources to you? What an impact that could have on your business!

Of course, you're probably already getting some referrals from past customers and contacts. But what if you made networking for referrals a major part of your overall client development strategy?

In this chapter, you'll find out how referral groups work, how to pick one or start one, how to make yours succeed, how to plan activities to help members get to know each other's business, and how to do the right things—and avoid the pitfalls—so that you reap the benefits.

See How They Run

It's 7 a.m. Members gulp coffee and gobble bagels. By 7:15, they're getting down to business. First, they take turns introducing themselves and their businesses. Next, three members present ten-minute briefings on their products or services. The travel agent drapes a lei around the shoulders of her business suit and tells about her new Hawaiian package tour. A handyman describes how he saved the day for a homeowner who frantically called him from work after a neighbor noticed an ominous stream of water gushing forth under the garage door. A stockbroker talks about the trends he sees and why international stocks are a growing part of most portfolios.

After the briefings, members—who have already been to the

bank with the income from business referred to them *by* other members or business *from* other members—jump up to say thanks. People also give thanks for resources, business advice, and valuable contacts. New referrals are exchanged. By 8:15, members are heading for their offices or businesses.

We tracked the progress of one group of seventy people over a one-year period. The dollars reported ranged from a low of $3,100 worth of referred business in one week to more than $94,000. (OK, there's a Lexus dealer in the group who got the lion's share of that week's business!)

"I got 25 percent of my business through the network last year," says Bob, a commercial photographer. His group is a nonprofit organization in Virginia that grew out of several local business and community groups. Participants are required to provide a total of at least twenty leads a year for others in the organization, which meets every other week. "That puts everyone in the group on your sales force," Bob says.

Many referral clubs are run as profit-making businesses. You pay an entry fee and monthly charges to participate. Look on the Internet under "Business Referral Clubs" to find out more about charges, benefits, and requirements.

In local chapters of Ali Lasen's Leads Clubs, business owners, sales people, managers, and professionals give brief presentations and exchange leads. The Clubs offer workshops on networking, a free newsletter, and ways to advertise your business.

Business Network International (BNI) provides a structured and supportive system of giving and receiving business. The founder, Ivan Misner, claims that some participants have added as many as fifty new clients in the first two years! BNI points out that you might spend as much as $2,000 for a one-time newspaper ad. But with a small membership fee, a local BNI club can turn thirty or forty other club members into your own sales force. Their statistics assert that the average member gives about forty-five leads per year. BNI has chapters in many countries around the world, from Malaysia to Sweden.

One of the members is Vincent, a builder in Van Nuys, California. Leads from a real estate broker in his chapter, who recommended him for two remodeling jobs, brought him $90,000 worth of work. The added business is great, says Vincent, but more important to the long-term growth of his firm are the networking skills he has gained. "I'm a better networker now just because I spend time doing it," he says.

PowerCore, based in Atlanta, has forty-two referral clubs with 717 members in the Atlanta metro area. Founded by Wendy Kinney, PowerCore's process gets results. A unique internal mentoring program called PowerLinks helps new members get connected. Power-Partners and coaches also are active in helping new members get up to speed fast. Kinney offers special workshops, free to members, to help them develop referral networking skills and self-promotion skills.

Three types of businesses benefit the most from PowerCore referral groups, reports Kinney: highly competitive businesses (such as real estate, insurance, remodeling); service or information-based businesses (including Web designers, CPAs, dentists, attorneys, and printers); and businesses that are so new or unique that potential customers don't even know they exist (including virtual assistants, professional organizers, and home stagers).

Conrad, a former Naval officer turned real estate agent, attributes more than $60,000 in commissions to referrals from his PowerCore Team in his second year of membership. Lucy, who sells nutritional supplements finds that the continued contact at weekly PowerCore meetings helps her break through the negative image some people have of network marketing companies like the one she's involved with. Terry, who owns a franchise business, raves that in his first year with the group, 10 percent of all his business came through PowerCore. In his second year of involvement that figure leaped to 21 percent. Robert, who's new in the insurance business, booked more than 30 percent of his business through his Team in his first year. Tracy, an interior designer, reports that half of her new clients in the last six months have come from her Team referrals.

Shop Around

Shop around until you find a group that meets your needs. To find groups, ask people in your network. Sometimes, groups are sponsored by Chambers of Commerce or government small business development agencies. Others are the brainchildren of individual business people. One very successful club in Maryland was started by a bridal consultant and a stockbroker. Watch your newspaper for meeting notices. Check with your library to see if it has a list of groups. Call the Chamber of Commerce. Inquire at local business support centers run by universities or community colleges, or ask the Small Business Administration.

New groups are springing up and membership in established groups is booming. The variety of formats and systems is amazing. The cost of membership in a club varies widely. Some groups charge an initial entry fee. Others just charge per meeting. Some charge enough to fund joint advertising projects or a newsletter to help members get to know each other. Non-profit groups may charge only for refreshments. Others include the price of breakfast or lunch. Some charge only when you show up. Others require that you pay three to six months in advance. Some groups meet in a restaurant or hotel. Others find meeting space at the office or store of a member to keep costs down. Find a model that works for you.

Find the referral group that's right fo you.

One group in Arizona has 146 members; other groups swear that a membership of twelve to fifteen people is optimal. Most groups allow only one of each kind of business to participate. That means, for instance, that one travel agent isn't competing against another travel agent in the group. Other groups allow anyone to join. Some groups carefully track and report on every lead given and taken. Other groups are much more informal and still get results.

The Arizona group teaches its members to say, "I'm a resource for anything you need." Members hand out each other's cards. Even though the group is very large, smaller Success Teams, made up of four to six people, get together each week for lunch. They know that learning more about how to help each other is a prerequisite for success.

Most referral groups publish some kind of membership roster, brochure, or flyer for members to give to their clients whenever appropriate. One Maryland group publishes a newsletter that introduces both members and prospects to the businesses. That group has also tried some joint advertising, using the theme, "Do business with people you trust."

Can your business profit from a referral group? Some types of businesses tend to achieve quicker results—referrals—than others. Caterers, gift services, bridal consultants, travel agents, printers, and florists are examples of businesses that do well. Accountants, lawyers, architects, doctors, and financial planners must be more patient to make their memberships pay off.

The amount of trust it takes to turn over your financial future to someone is much greater than the trust it takes to turn over the printing of your next business card. Remember too, that the dollar amounts of the referrals vary greatly. Dave, a real estate agent, passed along a remodeling job to Chuck that eventually netted $62,000. LeeAnn, a computer consultant, gave Jerry a lead for his advertising specialties business that resulted in an order for twenty T-shirts, with a $300 value.

The most effective groups recognize that three ingredients build strong referral groups:

1. *The Quality of Members.* Choose people who are known for their Character and Competence.

2. *The Quality of the Referrals.* Give leads that are qualified and preferably come with a personal introduction from you.

3. *The Quality of the Members' Networking Skills.* Teach members how to cultivate relationships and pro-actively look for business opportunities for each other.

Check It Out

Investigate groups before you join. Find out about:

1. *Membership and Other Fees.* Low-cost groups may be as effective as high-cost groups.

2. *Attendance Rules.* Some groups ask members who miss a certain number of meetings to give up their seat to someone else in that business category.

3. *Expectations About How Many Leads a Member Must Provide.* How much pressure is there to produce? Sometimes the quality of the leads diminishes when people are hounded for quantity.

4. *Time Commitments.* In addition to the scheduled meetings, how much additional time is required?

5. *Leadership Responsibilities.* Will you be expected to serve on committees?

6. *Entrance Requirements.* Are there rules about the size of your business or how long you have been in business?

7. *Categories of Businesses in the Group.* Is the group non-competitive, with only one member per category?

8. *What Members Say About the Group's Value.* What's the turnover?

9. *The Group's Reputation in the Business Community.* What do people think of the group?

10. *The Group's Track Record.* How long has the group has been in existence? What bottom-line value do members place on their participation?

Don't Just Join, Join In

Once you sign up, take your share of responsibility for making the group an effective referral source for you. Here are some guidelines for participating:

▶ Be there. If you don't attend—every time—you won't reap the benefits.

▶ Give it time. Referral group leaders say it takes a year for your business to begin getting the number and kind of referrals that make a big difference in your bottom line. Advertising gurus say prospects must hear or see your message nine times before they become customers. And, since prospects aren't really paying attention two-thirds of the time, it takes twenty-seven exposures to make nine impressions. If your group meets every other week, that's a year's worth of "exposures" before your message will sink in.

▶ Create sound bites. As you introduce yourself week after week, focus on the different aspects of your business and attach a one or two-sentence Success Story to give a vivid example.

Don, VP of sales and marketing for a temporary agency, never introduces himself with his title. Instead, he says things like, "We screen our temporaries—screen like we're panning for gold. Last week, a customer called me and said, 'We made our project deadline, thanks to the incredible people you sent us,'" or "Do you need an extra pair of hands? My agency can send you people who are experts on any of eighteen different software packages," or "We're the people-power people." Sometimes, Don holds up a paper doll he bought at a party supply store. As he talks, he pulls that one paper doll out into a string of twenty-five, and says, "Whatever you're short of, we have someone with that skill who can be there within 24 hours. Yesterday, I filled a request for a bilingual receptionist in less than three hours."

▶ Help the group grow. Bring prospective members whose businesses represent unfilled categories. If your group doesn't have a photographer, find one who'd be interested in joining and whose expertise and business practices would reflect well on you and the other members. Be alert for prospective members whose customers might need your services also. If you build decks, find a landscaper. The homeowner who is interested in putting in a rock garden might also want a new deck.

▶ Demonstrate your Character and Competence. In everything you do and say, show people they can trust you. Then, they won't hesitate to refer you to one of their customers or friends.

▶ Get together in ever-changing groups of three or four outside the referral group meeting to learn more about how you can help each other get business.

▶ Tell people how they can help you and who your ideal clients are.

▶ Listen Generously so that you know what kinds of information or leads to give. The Reciprocity Principle *does* work. If you give, you will receive.

►Ask others in the group for feedback about how you introduce yourself and how you describe your business. Others will help you refine what you say to make it as effective as possible.

►Encourage the group to provide books or training programs or hire networking specialists to do workshops to enhance member's skills.

►Practice all of the networking skills in this book and teach them to others.

Start Small

To speed your success, do one-month blitzes. Put together Success Teams of four or five members, and use these ideas to strengthen your relationships quickly. Next month, create new teams. Here are twelve ideas for Success Teams:

1. Meet several times. Eat lunch or breakfast together.

2. Give each teammate ten of your business cards to hand out to potential clients or customers.

3. "Test" each other to make sure *each one of you* can describe—accurately and vividly—exactly what your teammates have to offer.

4. Visit each other's places of business.

5. Ask each member of the team to describe in detail his ideal customer (or an actual customer) so that you know who each person is looking for.

6. Ask each teammate to tell you about a current business or personal challenge and do everything in your power to assist him or her in coming up with a solution.

7. Designate a spokesperson to share your team's experience with the rest of the members at a regular meeting of the referral group.

8. Talk about where you might find or run across people to refer your teammates to. Keep the idea of referrals at the top of your mind.

9. Ask each teammate to tell stories about satisfied customers or clients. Why exactly, were they so happy with the team member's product or service?

10. Provide a special incentive for teammates to try your product or service and to experience how good you are!

11. Brainstorm with your teammates how else you might be able to help each other.

12. Teach these activities to others in the referral group.

Spice Up the Meetings

After several months, Jan's group was getting stale. The steering committee decided it was time to change the meeting format and wake people up. They decided to start off every meeting with three, five-minute one-on-one's. In pairs, members were asked to discuss questions that would nudge them out of "Ho-hum" and into "No kidding!"

Here are the questions they used over several months:

▶How did you get started doing what you do? Why are you in the business you're in?

▶Where is your place of business? Is it easily accessible? Can you describe how to get there from here? Is it the best place for your business to be? Pros and cons?

▶What's your problem/concern/challenge today or this week? Brainstorm possible resources or solutions with your partner.

▶What's your unique capability? What do you do that most others in your line of work don't do? If you don't have a unique capability, what could it be?

▶Describe a recent satisfied customer. How do you know the person was satisfied?

▶If you had a smart person to help you all day today, what would you have that person do?

▶What one thing gets you down? What do you do to get "up" again?

►What's the one reason for your success so far? What have you done right?

►What's the best mistake you ever made—the one that you learned the most from?

►What would you like to quit doing in your business?

►What would you like to start doing in your business?

►If money were no obstacle, what do you need to improve your business?

►What other two member's businesses are most compatible with yours? For example, which businesses target the same customers?

►What did you learn in school that is not true?

►What did your mom/dad tell you that is true?

►What's your best marketing tool?

►What would you like a prospective customer to hear about your business?

►What motivates you?

►What do you get the biggest kick out of?

►When is your slowest time of the year? What do you do about that?

Start Your Own

Some groups struggle along. Perhaps too many of the members are start-ups. Perhaps turnover is high because people have unrealistic expectations about the amount of business they'll get—and how quickly. Some people don't understand the need for trust and expect instant referrals. Perhaps the group is *supposed* to be a referral group, but spends a lot of its time listening to programs about topics irrelevant to members' business growth. (One group's newsletter listed the following programs: What's New at the Zoo, Afghanistan Today, and The Responsibility of the Media in a Democratic Society!) Perhaps people just plain don't have the networking skills it takes to be good referrers. If you are involved with a struggling group, don't assume the *idea* doesn't work; assume that the *group* doesn't work. One solution is to start your own.

There are pros and cons to starting your own referral group. The biggest plus is that you can handpick members, rather than link up with an already established group of people. Another benefit of starting your own group is that you'll have lots of input to design a meeting format that gives you maximum interaction. If you put together a small steering committee, there will be several of you to handle the finances, find the meeting place, and set ground rules— all important (but time-consuming) activities.

The design of some groups shows real strategic genius. The president of a security systems company carefully teaches his salespeople, who are scattered throughout the country, how to start their own referral groups. He shows them how to select the core group, so that members are from businesses that serve customers who will probably also need burglar alarms and fire safety equipment.

Remember, whether you join a group or start your own, each group has a personality, a reputation, a networking culture. Make yours upbeat, generous, friendly, and professional.

CHAPTER 19

Connect at Conventions

What's so hard about going to a convention? You send in your registration, buy your plane ticket, pack your suitcase, and go. Right?

Well, that's the way *most* people go to conventions. But what you actually gain from a conference depends on how you interact with the other attendees. You could read a book or professional journal and get virtually the same information you'll receive from attending a convention. The difference, though, is obvious. A conference brings people face-to-face. If you don't make effective contact with the other people at the convention, you'll go home feeling vaguely dissatisfied.

Amazingly, there are shelves and shelves of books in the library devoted to *planning* meetings and conventions. But there are no books on how to be an effective participant. Use the ideas in this chapter for what to do before, during, and after the conference. You can make conventions valuable business experiences that are worth your time and effort.

Expand Your Expectations

Contacts Count surveys show that attendees and their bosses expect three things from the conference experience: information, inspiration, and interaction.

221

The meeting planner designs the program to accomplish the first two. Without taking much initiative, you'll soak up information and inspiration as you attend the sessions and listen to the speakers. But generating the one-on-one connections that enrich and expand that knowledge and motivation is, for the most part, up to you. It's your responsibility to create the individual interactions that make the time and money spent worthwhile.

Bringing people together face-to-face is expensive. In the business community, there are periodic efforts to replace meetings with video or Web teleconferencing. On the other hand, there are strong arguments for convening in person. Your organization will be more eager to pay for you to attend conventions, if you can bring back bottom-line benefits. Use the tips in the rest of this chapter for planning ahead, connecting at the conference, following up when you're back at work, and justifying the expense.

Get Ready, Get Set, Before You Go

Take these steps to get ready.

Set your Agenda. Make a written list of your To Gives and To Gets. By making an Agenda, you customize the conference so that it exactly meets your needs. (See Chapter 10 for specific instructions on making Agendas.)

On the To Give side, jot down things to share with the people you meet:

▶ New resources you've discovered.

▶ Special expertise you've developed.

▶ Problems you've solved.

▶ Successes you've had.

Even if you are a newcomer, you still have insights and enthusiasms you might offer.

If you are a veteran, make a note about information you can provide to those just coming into the field and about what will be on your Agenda when you talk with the other "old hands."

On the To Get side, go for the gold and make your list as long as possible. Jot down what you want to find:

►Answers to challenges you're facing.

►Solutions to problems you're dealing with.

►Resources you need to succeed.

►People you'd like to meet.

Martina is an independent consultant in human resources who focuses on pharmaceutical companies. Her convention Agenda included a variety of items, as shown in Figure 19-1.

Martina is ready for meaty conversations. When someone asks her, "How are you?" or "What's new?" she can turn to her Agenda for a topic. And if the person she's chatting with doesn't know about "overseas contracting," for example, Martina can ask, "Do you know anyone here I could talk to about that?" She'll probably be passed along to someone with that expertise.

Take along other people's Agendas. To build your relationships with colleagues, your boss, your sales people, or your business partner, collect their concerns and hunt for answers for them at the meeting.

After you are clear about your Agenda, tell people. Business

FIGURE 19-1. Agenda Items.

To Give	To Get
Experience with contact management software for keeping track of vendors, clients, associates.	A woodsy conference center with a relaxed atmosphere for a group of 200 managers.
The best training films on diversity from a vendor film festival she attended.	Information on retirement options in the Southwest.
Information on bidding and contracting with companies overseas.	How to find and apply for scholarships for college-age kids. (She has twins!)
Ideas for streamlining proposal writing.	How to market "soft skills" training to bottom-line companies.
Ideas on providing "Train the Trainer" programs and how to price them.	Access to several people who have recently published books to find out about their experiences and get their recommendations.

people often see conventions as "just a joy junket." Sell your attendance. Send a memo to key people in your organization telling them that you're going to the conference. Attach a copy of the program. Your colleagues may know some of the speakers and may be able to tell you, "Dr. Dud is a waste of time, but be sure to hear Ms. Up-and-Coming." Ask if there's anything you can do for the organization while you are in the convention's host city. Your memo also lets others in your company know you are serious about your professional development. Emphasize that your attendance is not just your annual trip to the Sunbelt, but an educational experience and a way to gather state-of-the-art strategies. Then report on the results when you return to work.

Choose your sessions in advance. Select your sessions before you arrive at your hotel room. Advance planning while you're still in the office will allow you to shape your experience to your goals. Select sessions carefully. Focus on the knowledge you need and the skills you want to develop. Look for the right sessions that will force you to reevaluate, plan for the future, and expand your horizons. Carefully pick a wild card session on a topic you think you may never have a use for. Invariably, that's the one that will open new doors for you or shine new light on old problems.

Divvy up sessions among several people from your organization who are attending or decide to attend one key session as a group and have a "How-are-we-going-to-apply-this?" get-together immediately afterward.

Begin to think about some topics that particularly interest you and to formulate the questions you'd like to ask at the session before you go.

Design your own sessions. Recognize that some of the best sessions are not listed in the conference brochure—they're set up by you! Arrange them *before* you leave for the conference. Here are some ideas. Visit a branch office or corporate headquarters to increase your knowledge of the business or to visit an internal customer. Meet with a key prospect or customer in the city where your conference is being held. Contact a speaker before the conference begins to suggest getting together for breakfast or lunch.

Set up a meeting with a board member, a guru, an expert, a counterpart from a similar organization, or colleague you've lost touch with. If a twosome seems intimidating, invite several people (they don't have to know each other!) to go out to dinner.

Before the meeting, Arnetta called a couple of acquaintances who were attending and invited them to dinner. At the conference when she met someone new or saw a colleague, she said, "I'm getting together a bunch of people to eat dinner at a great Italian restaurant. If you'd like to come, meet in the lobby at 6:30." Arnetta's sense of adventure was contagious. Nine people showed up and enjoyed a leisurely dinner exploring connections and common challenges.

Plan an out-of-the-ordinary experience to stimulate your creativity. That experience might have a business payoff. At a convention in New Orleans, Don took a guided tour of jazz spots. Six months later, he was producing a video program for his company and searching for appropriate music. A blues tune he'd heard in one of the jazz joints popped into his mind. His video later won an award. In Orlando, while other conventioneers were at Disney World, Jenna visited a shelter for homeless women. She got excited about a program that encourages employees to donate clothes so the women from the shelter can dress appropriately for job interviews. When she started a similar program back home, she improved life for others and gained positive PR for her image consulting business.

Build in time to relax, unwind, exercise, and see the sights. Seek out information about the city before you go. Look at the city's home page on the Internet. Also browse though travel magazines. How can you take advantage of the location of the conference? If you don't find ways to take advantage of the site, you might as well be staying at home. What new things do you want to see? Plan ahead to use recreation—or even regional cuisine—to stimulate your creativity.

Volunteer for a job at the conference. Call ahead and offer to help out. Find the name of the chairperson of a committee on which you'd like to serve, and volunteer your talents. It's a rare group that can't use an extra pair of hands. You'll find it easy to make contact with people that way. You'll also gain professional visibility, mingle with the leaders, and build a nationwide network.

Or give *yourself* a job to do at the conference. Before you leave home, arrange to bring back a report on some aspect of the conference to a person in your organization, to your company newspaper, to your city newspaper, or to your local professional group. Having a job to do will strengthen your Agenda, and you'll feel as if you have an even better reason to meet people, ask questions, and take notes.

Show Up at the Conference

Be there! Set aside thoughts of the work stacking up back on your desk and the messages piling up in your e-mail inbox. Use these ten tips for making great convention connections.

1. *Arrive at the convention early.* The important people— speakers, conference organizers, association leaders—are likely to arrive early for "pre-meeting meetings." Rub shoulders with the successful people. They are the ones with the connections. Find a mentor or a role model.

2. *Wear a smile.* Make your body language say, "I'd be easy to talk to." React to visual clues. Comment on jewelry, a necktie, a T-shirt, a nametag listing a state you've traveled in. If you're in line to pick up theater tickets with someone who is wearing the same kind of convention badge you are, go with the obvious. Say, "Hi, I'm Jack, Jack Armstrong. I'm at the NCAC convention, too."

3. *Volunteer (again!) to help.* Give out nametags, fill in for a panelist whose plane got fogged in, distribute hand-outs for the speaker. Participation leads to relationships.

4. *Take advantage of the "meetings in the hallway."* Make the most of all the informal and unstructured moments. Introduce yourself to someone sitting near you before the keynoter begins to speak. Strike up a conversation with someone in the hotel lobby or at a luncheon. Welcome a newcomer. Congratulate a new board member at the opening reception. If you meet just one person who can help you boost your sales, advance your career, land a new job, or solve a problem that's festering back on your desk, you'll call the convention a success.

5. ***Introduce yourself to speakers or panelists.*** Welcome them before the program, and let them know why you chose their session. Often, they are eager for more information on who's in the audience, so if they aren't busy getting ready, talk to them. They may mention you in their presentation—instant visibility! Or talk to the speaker afterwards. Ask if he or she is free for coffee or lunch to continue the discussion. It's rare to be turned down. If people can't do what you ask, they may offer something even better in return. One speaker said to Robert, "I can't go to lunch right now, but why don't you join Wolf and me for supper." Wolf turned out to be CNN anchorman Wolf Blitzer! If you feel shy about issuing an invitation to a speaker, ask two or three other people with similar interests to lunch and then ask the speaker to join the group.

6. ***Participate in the sessions.*** Ask a question. This does several things. It forces you to think actively rather than just sitting passively and taking it all in. When you speak, stand and talk loud enough to be heard. Introduce yourself and tell where you're from or what organization you're with. You'll be remembered because you have been seen. Your visibility makes it easier for people to come up to you after the session and start a conversation. If there is time, you might even announce that you'd like to talk to people who "have successfully used an executive search firm" or "have solved the problem of doing long-distance sales training when field offices are spread out"—whatever is on your Agenda. Your question may attract others who have the same interests. Also, listen carefully to other people's questions. Follow up after the session by getting with those people, commenting on their questions or asking more about their point of view. Those are instant conversation starters.

7. ***Sit with strangers.*** At sessions and meals, don't sit with people you already know. Use that time to meet someone new. Tell yourself that there are no accidental meetings, and try to figure out what you and the other person have in common. Find out what others are looking for and help them connect with resources and contacts.

8. *Look for excuses to introduce people to each other.* Listen for commonalties, then be a great connector. "Fred, I want you to meet Sam. You both are in charge of leadership development programs in your organizations." "Mary, I want you to meet Sunita. You both are program chairs for your chapters. I know you'll have lots to talk about!"

9. *Consult the list.* You may receive a list of attendees in your registration packet. Use it to look for people you'd like to meet. Take every opportunity to start conversations. Welcome first-timers. Thank an association leader for his or her hard work. Say hello in the elevators. Meet people who have the kind of job you have now. Meet others who have the kind of job you think you'd like to have next. Meet people from your own geographical area. Discuss regional or state activities. You might find out about new activities you'd like to take part in; or if you're already active, you might enlist an enthusiastic new member for your regional, state, or local organization. Your Agenda will give you ready-made topics.

10. *Be prepared to job hunt—even if you don't think you're looking for a job.* Update your resumé and take a dozen copies with you. Make sure your business cards are up to date. Put together a few samples of your work. If there is a placement service, sign up and set up interviews with prospective employers to practice your interviewing skills. Throw in a U.S. map. You may want to be able to locate Bigville on the map. Interviewing gives you an idea of your marketability and the going rate in other parts of the country for the kind of work you do. If you are in the process of hiring, interview people for your job opening. Even if you don't fill the job with a person you interviewed at the conference, you'll have a benchmark against which to measure the people you interview when you return home. You also may be able to pick up a job description for a job you are creating. Then you won't have to write one from scratch.

Follow Up After You Get Home

Sit down at your computer with your notes, and compile a list of major ideas, resources, and contacts. Turn sketchy notes into action steps. Make a list of people to Follow Through with. Do it within a week. Did you promise to send your counterpart, a franchisee in Albuquerque, that interesting article on selling to baby boomers? Do it! Did you say you'd review someone's resumé and send it back? Do it!

Tell your boss about the conference. Then follow up with a memo. Pass along all of the exciting ideas you heard. Tell the boss who you talked to, what sessions you attended, what you learned, and why it's valuable to you and the organization.

It's a great opportunity to meet with the people in your company you asked for advice or who gave you a job to do. Translate what you learned into positive observations, suggestions, or plans for your company or organization.

Go ahead and write that article for your company newspaper. Your fellow employees might be fascinated to hear what the keynote speaker, filmmaker Ken Burns, said about leadership. Of course, if you're really gutsy, you will have gone up to him and asked him for any experiences he's had that would especially apply to your industry.

Take a tip from Beth. As she was sorting through all the cards she received at the national convention, she reread the notes she'd made on the backs. Then, she hit on another idea. She pulled out her association directory and highlighted in yellow all the folks she'd met. She tagged them with sticky notes—yellow for members and blue for vendors. She copied the notes from the backs of the cards into the directory and refreshed the name/face connection. Next year, when she goes to the convention, she'll pack the book or tear out the highlighted pages and take them with her.

Later On, Get Re-Inspired

Finally, six months later, take out your notes and re-read them. Choose a rotten, rainy Monday morning for this exercise. You'll find that all the ideas and enthusiasm and inspiration you felt while you were at the convention come flooding back. That's what a convention is for: To give you ideas and to stimulate you. William James, the psychologist, was talking once about the time it takes for the unconscious to incubate ideas. He said, "We learn to swim in the winter and skate in the summer." You may find that ideas from the conference have now incubated and are ready to be hatched.

Also, at this six-month point, send notes to some of the people you talked with at the last convention. Ask them if they are going to be attending the next one. Keep in touch with your contacts. Put them on your holiday card list. That will make going to the next conference much easier: You'll be looking forward to seeing, not strangers, but your valuable business contacts.

Assess how well you did at focusing on your Agenda. Did you answer your questions? Did you solve the problems you took with you to the conference? Did you meet many of the people you wanted to meet? If you can say yes, then you have succeeded at the art of conventioneering.

Bonus: Plan Meetings That Get People Talking

Chances are that sometime, somewhere, you'll be involved in planning a convention, a sales kick-off, a regional conference, or a meeting for a local group. The sessions may be fantastic, the food may be delicious, the hotel may rate five stars, but what brings people back are the connections they make at the meeting you are in charge of. Look at Figure 19-2 for some more tips.

Here are twelve ideas to increase the interaction.

1. *Prepare attendees before the conference*. Put articles and tip sheets on "networking know-how" in your magazine, newsletter, and convention publicity/registration packets. Make the "netiquette" of making contact in this organization crystal clear. That will give attendees the confidence to go from casual conversations to great connections.

2. *Make nametags novel.* Print first names BIG. As conversation starters, add special ribbons or colored stickers designating interests to help people find each other.

3. *Give out several blank nametags.* Tell people to wear a new one each day and write on it something they're eager to talk with others about. Or pre-print nametags to say, "Talk to me about . . ." and ask attendees to write in a topic they want or need to talk about. Agenda-based nametags make opening conversations easier.

FIGURE 19-2. Meetings That Get People Talking.

No-Nos	Know-Hows
Hope they are comfortable connecting.	Teach the "rules and tools" of networking, with special pre-conference materials.
Assume they have an Agenda.	Give pre-conference and onsite aid and encouragement so that people create new Agendas every day.
Print too much or too small on nametags.	Print bold and colorful first names.
Leave newcomers on their own.	Get great greeters!
Think they want polite chit-chat at meals.	Suggest Table Talk Topics at some meals.
Expect speakers to know how to get people talking.	Show them how to encourage small groups and "in the hallway" follow-ups.
Assume people will find each other.	Offer many small "meetings within the meeting."
Hope people will stay in touch.	Give them reasons and tools.
Wonder how it went.	Do focus groups and e-mail surveys to find out.

4. *Maximize the mix and mingle.* Include some short, structured, one-on-ones or threesomes to encourage mixing and meeting. Choose an energetic, well-known person to lead the session. Plan the questions carefully to fit the group's interests and culture.

5. *Manage the music.* Use music to energize or entertain, but keep the volume low and don't let it compete with conversation. People will leave your expensive reception in droves if they can't hear each other!

6. *Give a hand for hospitality.* Train leaders, staff, and volunteers how to introduce people to each other. Teach them how to encourage conversations at mixers and sessions. Invite people to go out to dinner or attend special events.

7. *Give people a way to begin conversations.* As they come into a session, pose a provocative question or topic on the screen and invite people to chat about it until the session starts.

8. *Spark up your speakers.* Remind speakers that attendees want to talk with each other, as well as listen to experts. Suggest ways for speakers to include some interaction in their sessions. Also invent ways for speakers to meet attendees. Encourage speakers to attend receptions and meals where attendees can talk informally with them.

9. *Make the most of meals.* Table talk isn't easy when the room is noisy and the tables are set for eight to ten. Work with the hotel on noise control and request smaller tables of four to six whenever possible. Using a Table Talk Host, or simply a bold sign at each table, suggest a topic or issue people can discuss over lunch. Topics that generate a lot of energy are ethical issues, future trends, or what's going on in local chapters. On "free" nights, invite people to sign up to go out to dinner in small groups. Designate a restaurant, host/hostess, and meeting place. Announce a "Lunch Bunch" for first-timers, people interested in certification, or people who want to swap tips on doing research on the Internet, etc.

10. *Schedule small success groups.* Create small group meetings or rap sessions around topics of interest. Give time for the groups to meet two or three times during the conference, then by e-mail during the year. Offer a "Meet the Pros" session. Attendees sign up in advance for 30-minute round table discussions with a "pro," who talks and answers questions about a pre-announced issue or topic.

11. *Foster follow up.* Be bold about suggesting how people can follow up and stay in touch after the meeting—on the Internet, with conference calls, at regional or special interest group meetings.

12. *Find out with a focus group.* Ask attendees, "How could we make this a more network-friendly event?" Interview them at a breakfast focus group or with an e-mail poll. Trust them to tell you what helps them get the interaction they came for.

CHAPTER 20

Jump-Start Your Job Hunt

If you're looking for a job, you probably opened to this chapter first. Good! We'll help you switch career fields, re-enter the job market after taking time off, get your first job after graduating, bounce back from a layoff, transition from military to civilian life, find new options and new directions, advance in your career field, or just find a better job faster—no matter what your current situation.

Whether your job change is voluntary or necessary, networking know-how is the key to your success. The length of your job search is inversely related to the strength of your network.

The stronger your network, the shorter your job search. The weaker your network, the longer your job search. Two-thirds of job-finders say they found their jobs through networking. As you apply The Contacts Count Networking System, you'll be able to create a circle of contacts that will give you "hot information" on openings; access to people you need to know; resources and services you must have to conduct your job search; and support to boost your spirits along the way. As you use the Twenty-Five Tactics to Find a Job Fast, you'll be confident that you are going about your job search in the most professional and efficient way.

Use the Contacts Count Networking System

Read this chapter to see how the four parts of The Contacts Count Networking System can help you jumpstart your job search. Then

233

start at the beginning of this book. Learn everything you need to know to be well equipped to use networking as your primary job-hunting tool.

1. *Survey your skills and your mindset.* What do you really know about networking? Taking the Self-Assessment in Chapter 1 will help you see which skills you've mastered and which ones you need to bone up on. You'll want to become so skillful a networker that connecting—comfortably and professionally—becomes a way of life for you. If you lack relationship-building skills, job hunting becomes a stressful and artificial process of sending out resumés and giving out business cards to strangers. Imagine the difference when your contacts want to help you!

Then, using Chapter 2, take a hard look at the attitudes and beliefs you have about networking. Choose a mindset that will make you more comfortable reaching out to people, even though, as a job-seeker, you feel in dire need of contacts.

2. *Set your strategy.* As you network to job hunt, there are two key concepts you must understand—how to teach people to trust you and how to intensify and deepen your relationships. See Chapters 3 and 4. If you don't know and use these concepts, your contacts will be superficial and a lot less likely to provide valuable assistance.

Assessing the state of your current network—how much time and money you're spending and what groups you're already connected to—will help you set your goals. You'll find that, as you network, you will arrive at many ChoicePoints—opportunities to make strategic decisions about what you'll do or say. And you'll find that thinking of your job hunt as a Strategic Positioning Project will give you an edge. See Chapter 5.

3. *Sharpen your skills.* Use your results on the Self-Assessment to guide you as you decide which skills to tackle first. But be aware that the skill chapters take you from Hello to Follow Though, so it makes sense to work your way through all of them. We guarantee that even the most sophisticated networker will discover plenty of new ideas. Need more help to get up to speed fast? Find a role model. Hire a coach. Enroll in a Contacts Count workshop or online session. Do whatever it takes, so your superior networking skills

make it possible for you to feel relaxed and competent, whatever the situation.

4. *Select your settings.* If you want to change jobs, you may need the information about networking inside your organization in Chapter 14. If you must find a job, you'll discover in Chapter 17 that not all networking venues are equal in the opportunities they can provide to a job hunter. You'll get help figuring out the best organizations to become active in—and how to up your visibility instantly. It's tempting, if you're out of work and paring expenses to the bone, to cut out membership dues. Don't do it. You'd be cutting off your lifeline to job banks that focus on your occupation, mentoring from the best and brightest in your field, professional development that you can add to your resumé, and access to fellow members who are predisposed to help you. Think about the benefits to you of attending a conference. Where else could you find that number of potential contacts? See Chapter 19 for ways to capitalize on your conference experience.

Twenty-Five Tactics to Find a Job Fast

Use these tactics to succeed with your job search networking Project.

1. *Talk to yourself.* This tactic will support you as you get ready to present yourself in a positive way. We know that it works and that it's essential. For twenty days, write for twenty minutes. Get in touch with your feelings—especially if you have been laid off. Pour out on the pages your challenges, frustrations, and fears, and get rid of your feelings of betrayal, and loss, and even guilt. Don't use this time to make plans and lists for your job hunt. As you jettison the junk in your head this way, you'll get unstuck and be ready to move on. If you don't let go of this stuff, it will drag you down.

2. *Know who you are.* If your job is everything and you lose it, who are you? It's not fair or true, but in this society we often get hooked into thinking we are our job titles, and if you haven't got one, you're nobody. The truth is that your job is what you do, not who you are. Since several of your job changes will be involuntary, as the result of downsizings, mergers, or moves, you'll be wise to

separate who you are from what you do. Vow now, as you job hunt, to develop a strong identity for yourself outside of your work—as a fundraiser for the Boy Scouts, for example, or as board member of a charitable organization. Start now as you are job hunting. Find at least one activity where you can excel and feel good about yourself and your talents. Be aware that good networking contacts often come from these extracurricular activities where you've had a chance to show what you can do.

3. *Enlist your family's support.* As you begin networking to find a job, don't overlook your own family. It's a low stress, low risk place to begin. As you talk to your near and dear, go though your resumé and practice saying what you are looking for. Ask relatives about their circles of contacts. You might find that your brother-in-law's father can introduce you to a key person.

4. *Update your business card.* Maybe you've been laid off or are reluctant to use the business card from your current organization because you want to develop a new career identity. So get a new one. Include all the standard identifiers on your new card, including your special career designations or certifications, and a few words about your skills. Carla used "Financial Manager" and a special e-mail address and a special website on which she posted her resumé and accomplishments. Bradley used "Computer Security Operations and Disaster Recovery," CISSP (his earned designation of Certified Information Systems Security Professional), and a cell phone number he got to handle all his job search calls.

Why not have several cards? They are easy to make on your computer or order at an office supply store. They help you teach people about your multiple job search identities. Laura was looking for advancement in her field as a marketer of new products. One card stressed her expertise as a professional manager of marketing teams; the other described her as a New Product Marketing Strategist.

5. *Join or start a job-hunting strategy and support group.* Job-hunting is lonely. People who link up with others keep their spirits up and learn from each other. You can find these groups sponsored by religious organizations, adult education centers, or women's centers. If you can't find a group, start one. See the Bonus section at the end of this chapter for tips. At one meeting, the group helped

Gary brainstorm ways to develop contacts in a certain company and think through his answer to the tricky job interview question: "How much are you willing to travel?" The group listened while Monica fumed about companies that granted her interviews, then never let her know when they postponed hiring or filled the job. The group role-played with Jack to help him put his best foot forward as he prepared for an interview in a field he wanted to switch to, but lacked a lot of direct experience in.

6. *Choose twenty organizations.* To focus your job search, choose twenty organizations you could imagine working for. Make your choices based on the organizations' locations, benefits plans, missions, predicted growth, or just because you have friends who work there. Set up a manila folder for each company and begin to fill it with every bit of "intelligence" you can find. Look on these companies' websites, order their annual reports, scan the newspaper and trade journals for articles about them. Most important, make the goal of your networking to build relationships with people in these twenty companies—or people who know people in these companies. Look through your network to see whom you already know people who might provide access or have tips for you. You'll hear about a job opening before it is announced, and you'll feel like an insider in the job interview because you'll know the company's history, trends, goals, culture, and practices.

7. *Select six Arenas.* Pull out the list of the Arenas you're already involved with. If you haven't yet made that list, see Chapter 5. Are you already active in six Arenas? Are they the right ones for your job search? If you are changing career fields, join an association that serves the job or industry you've targeted. Look over the hierarchy of networking opportunities in Chapter 17 to be sure you've got the right mix.

8. *Raise your visibility.* Now that you've joined, the work of building relationships and making yourself visible begins. Go to every meeting. Take advantage of everything the group has to offer. Get involved so people can see your talents. Use the networking portion of the meetings to find the people you want to know better. Visit the group's website. There may be an online directory that will help you pick out people you want to contact. Talk with members about what they do and how they got their jobs. Ask for their advice on conducting your job search.

9. *Pick fifty people.* You can't network with everybody, so choose fifty people for your job-hunt network. Start your list now. The more diverse your network, the better because, when you know people in a variety of Arenas and with a variety of backgrounds, they will hear about opportunities that you won't hear about. Your best job leads will come, not from who you know, but from who they know. Include those family members you talked with and people from the groups you belong to. If your list doesn't total fifty, think again. Include friends, neighbors, someone who serves with you on the condo Board of Directors, and selected alumni from your alma mater. Look for people who might know people in the twenty organizations you've targeted.

10. *Relocate the "information interview."* When coauthor Anne worked for a large corporation, she frequently got calls from people who were job hunting in Kansas City. They asked to talk with her about her job and the field of corporate communications. Anne's usual response was a tough one, but realistic. She'd say, "My company doesn't pay me to talk to you during my work day about my job or your job hunt." Then to soften the blow of that much candor—and because she did want to be helpful—she would invite the caller to attend her professional organization's monthly luncheon. She'd tell him she'd talk with him there and also make sure he met others in the field.

Be creative about when and where you do these interviews. Talk to people at a party, in your carpool, or at a convention. Don't assume that they can donate their company's time to talk with you.

11. *Teach people to trust you.* Two things teach that you are trustworthy: What you say and what you do.

Janna knew she'd see Joe, who works at a company she'd like to interview with, at the neighborhood barbecue on Saturday. She decided he'd trust her Competence more if she gave him some third party evidence of her success and expertise. She found a way to mention being asked to speak on a panel of experts about Ethics in the Workplace. Remember the All or Nothing Rule: If you do one thing well, people will assume that you do everything well.

12. *Observe the protocols.* Let your contact know your plans. If someone gives you information, tell the person what you intend to do with it. Don't jump the gun. Allow your contact to determine

the timing of what happens next or when you will follow through. "I casually mentioned a job opportunity I knew about to an unemployed acquaintance," says one executive. "I had planned, if she was interested, to phone my contact and arrange a meeting. Our telephone conversation was interrupted and when I called her back fifteen minutes later, she already had called my contact about the position, using me as a reference. I was very embarrassed. That job had been offered to me, and I had not yet refused it."

Pay your way. When you call a contact and ask that person to meet you for breakfast or lunch or a drink, the least you can do is offer to pay. Be sure also that you schedule the meeting at a location that's as convenient as possible for your contact. Dress appropriately for the meeting. Treat every meeting with every contact as a job interview. Remember that you are teaching your contacts who you are. Help them to see you in the position to which you aspire!

13. *Prepare an answer for "what do you do?"* Come up with several ways to answer this question. Avoid the mysterious "I'm in transition." Each answer should reflect a different talent you have, direction you'd like to go, or setting you'd like to work in. Each way should be vivid enough to make you memorable.

Marly, a veterinarian at the U.S. Department of Agriculture, used to give this answer: "I decide how many camels come into the U.S.. I just got back from Oman, and there are 300 on the way." But she realized she was becoming known as "The Camel Lady."

She wanted to leave her veterinary career behind and parlay the negotiating and language skills she'd learned bargaining about camels into a new career negotiating international contracts and agreements. So she changed her answer to, "I help people come to agreement. Last week, after months of patient coaching, I got six people who speak three different languages to sign contracts for their companies to work together." What she doesn't tell you is that these six people were talking about camels! With her new answer, she taught her contacts to see her in a new light—and to think of her when they heard of opportunities that could use her negotiating and language skills.

Raj, who wants to change from hospital personnel administration to directing a customer service improvement program in a healthcare organization, says, "I'm studying how hospitals can better serve their clients. I've just interviewed four experts for a presentation I'm giving next week at the American College of Healthcare Executives conference." When Benita was asked, "What do you do?" she didn't have an organization, but she had an answer. "I just won Salesperson of the Year from my firm because I increased my sales by 12 percent in a crowded market." What she didn't say was that three days earlier she had lost her job because her company moved to Phoenix! It's not that these job-seekers want to keep their job search a secret. Not at all. It's just that they want to bring it up at the right time, in the right way, after they've shown their Character and Competence.

14. *Broaden your outlook.* As you teach people what you're looking for, don't limit yourself to a specific title. Instead, aim to teach your contacts about your talents. Garth called Benjamin and said, "I'm looking for a position as a Chief Financial Officer." Benjamin told Garth he didn't know of any jobs for CFOs. A few days later, Benjamin heard about a fast-growing waste-management company that wanted to raise capital for expansion. He didn't think of passing that tip along to Garth because Garth hadn't let him know that he'd been very successful in his previous job at raising capital. Garth had made the mistake so many job-hunters make—restricting himself to one title.

15. *Give first.* As a job seeker, you may feel that you don't have anything to give. Not true! Before you go to a social or professional event, tune into the To Give side of your Agenda. As you talk with someone, Listen Generously and think, "Who do I know or what resources am I in touch with that my contact might benefit from?" When her husband's job transfer took Angela to San Antonio, she started her networking to find a job there from scratch. She met Lynn at the first American Business Women's Association meeting she attended. Lynn mentioned she was beginning her yearly search for the perfect summer camp for her eleven-year-old. Angela remembered an article she'd read reviewing local camps. She promised to send it to Lynn. What a good reason for exchanging cards! When Lynn called to say thanks, Angela told her more about the kind of job she was looking for, and Lynn gave her a lead.

Give first: Give freel

16. *Get exactly what you need.* Be prepared to ask for valuable information and resources. Fill out the To Get side of your Agenda

before you go anywhere. Approach each situation with a list of resources and information you're looking for. Then ask directly for what you need. Are you looking for people who work for those twenty companies? Ask people at a networking event. Or look for other information and resources you need. Ask, "Have you run across any information recently on negotiating salaries?" Or, "I'd like to start a Strategy and Support group with other people who are changing careers. Know anybody who might be interested?" Or, "I came here hoping to meet people who work in some aspect of health research. Do you know anyone who does that?" See Chapter 10 for tips about how to update your Agenda and guide your conversations.

17. *Ask stepping stone questions.* These are questions whose answers will get you moving in the right direction and that signal your creativity and diligence. It doesn't work to say to someone you've just met or who is an Associate or Actor in your network, "I'm looking for a job. Are there any openings at your company?" The problem is that you're asking your contact to go out on a limb for you before he knows much about you.

For Dana, who was looking for a job managing and editing association publications, a good Stepping Stone Question was, "Do you know anyone who's a member of the local chapter of the American Society of Association Executives here in town? I'd like to talk with someone in the group before I attend a meeting." Bret, who is transitioning to civilian life from a military career in procurement, doesn't ask for a job in purchasing. He asks, "Do you know of any companies that are buying heavy equipment or building new plants?" It's always good to ask for advice. An example: "If I wanted to work for your company, what are the top two qualities I'd have to have to get hired?" When you hear the answers, you can respond with stories that illustrate that you have those qualities.

18. *Immerse yourself in the culture.* Want to look like an insider by the time you get to the job interview? Spend time with people who have the job you'd like to have. As you volunteer for committees, go to certification classes, or attend conventions, notice what they read, how they dress, what they talk about, and who their gurus are. Listen for special terms company employees use to describe what they do.

Kevin was winding down his career in the Marine Corps. He had enrolled in an MBA program at a university near the base. As he got to know his classmates, he gathered information about their organizations. He listened to Jonas talk about the business benefits of playing on the company softball team and asked Al about the appropriate garb for "dress-down" days at his company and personnel hiring practices for ex-military.

Look for someone who will take you under his wing, answer questions, look over your resumé, give you advice, and introduce you to others. A mentor might be a friend who's already in the field, a past college professor, or someone you meet in a professional association. Many groups make getting a mentor easy by offering a formal program, complete with training for mentor and mentee.

Of course you can read about IBM, if that's one of the twenty corporations you chose when you planned your strategy. But the best way to get the scoop on the latest happenings is from people, not print. Review your list of fifty people. Who works for IBM? Who knows someone who works for IBM? Which organizations do you belong to that might have members who work for IBM? Who in your alumni association works there? Then look for ways to get into conversation with these people to learn all you can. Strategically build your network of people who are active in the Arena you've targeted.

19. *Work for free.* Offer to help someone. Mary Alice, a whiz with all kinds of graphics software packages, wanted to learn more about careers in corporate training, so she offered to create a brochure for the freelance trainer who lived next door. In the process, she picked up more knowledge of the field and demonstrated her expertise. Her relationship with the trainer eventually led to several introductions and a corporate job designing internal training materials. Mary Alice is now one step closer to her goal: making the transition into delivering training.

20. *Give yourself a job.* As a job-hunter, you may have more time, so take on high-visibility jobs others don't have time to do. After Bob was laid off, he attended a regional convention of his professional association that was taking place in his hometown and made

Showcase your skill to the people who count.

himself useful and visible. He manned the registration desk so he could greet people, introduced a prominent speaker to the group of 400, and drove a past president of the association to the airport. Soon after, the past president called with a job lead for him.

21. *Look for problems to solve.* Tom Jackson, prolific author on job-hunting techniques says, "A job is an opportunity to solve a problem—and there is no shortage of problems." Ask yourself, "What kinds of problems have I been most successful with?" When you describe what you do in terms of the problems you solve, you put a picture of success in people's minds. Listening for problems can give you ideas on how to describe the skills on your resumé in the exact language your prospective employer uses. When Linda heard Jake talk about his company's new initiative in "internal customer service," that's what she called her expertise in the cover letter and resumé she sent to him. Talking about problems you solve might even result in an organization inventing a job just for you.

22. *Don't make unreasonable, inappropriate requests.* Dan brought 100 copies of his resumé to the networking meeting, left some on the display table, and gave one to everybody he talked to, saying, "If you know anyone who needs my skills, ask them to call me." This is the kind of behavior that gives networking a bad name. Why would you take the chance of recommending Dan to anyone you know? You'd want to be sure of Dan's Character and Competence before telling your contacts and colleagues about him. His request was presumptuous.

23. *Fill in the blank spot on your resumé.* Take a university course or get an advanced degree. Education builds your credibility and puts you in touch with contacts who can help you.

Martha Lee had been out of the job market for thirteen years. She began a degree program at a university that was designed for working professionals. She arranged for an internship with the organization one of her professors worked for and later—after she'd proved herself—was hired part-time. Networking with classmates provided her with additional leads and opportunities.

Dottie hadn't planned on taking time off from work. Then she had twin boys. To keep herself current, she worked on her master's degree while she was at home with the boys for three years. When she did decide to look for a job, there was no gap on her resumé.

The time she had spent at home was "covered" by her pursuit of the advanced degree. She also networked with professors and classmates and quickly found a job.

24. *Say thanks.* Let people know how much you appreciate their time, information, and support. Do it throughout your job hunt and again when you find a job. To stand out, send hand-written notes. Tell your contacts what steps you took to put their help to use or how that information led to additional resources. Jan says, "My thank you cards are every bit as important as my business cards. I want people who help me move my job search along to know that I noticed and valued their efforts on my behalf." After you land a job, send one of your new business cards to your contacts.

25. *Network in your new job.* Once people get a job, they often make two mistakes. They think, "Whew! That's over. Now I can stop networking." Wrong! Your network must always be ready to act as a safety net. In today's uncertain economic climate—mergers, downsizing, reorganizations—you never know when you are really going to need your business and personal contacts. Or they think, "I'm so busy with my new responsibilities that I don't have time to network!" Sure, you want to get up to speed fast on

> Your network is you[r] safety net. Make su[re] it's in place before you need it.

the tasks you are expected to accomplish. But also spend time building relationships and setting up your network. Read Chapter 14 for tips on how to cultivate a wide circle of contacts, outside your department, as you start your new job. And go to www.FireProofYour Career.com for more tips about how networking can protect your career. Always be eager to stay and prepared to go.

Bonus: Manage Your Strategy Support Group

If you join or create a job search/career change strategy support group with others who are in transition, here's a process that works.

With this group you'll commiserate, celebrate, brainstorm, problem-solve, and make agreements about completing the sometimes challenging tasks that will help you find a job.

Meet every week or every other week. Limit the group to no more than five people. That way, each person will get the time he or she needs. Choose these people carefully to be sure they are positive and motivated. The group works best if each of you is looking for work in a different job function and or setting.

Before the meeting:

▶ In your private notebook, list all your accomplishments since your last meeting.

▶ List issues or challenges you want to discuss with the group.

At the meeting:

▶ Take twenty minutes to tell your accomplishments and get help with your challenges. Set a timer and stick to the allotted time for each person.

▶ When it's your turn to have the group's attention, tell your accomplishments, then tell the group what kind of help you'd like:

The Echo. "I need to talk in order to figure out where I am on this. I'll talk, you listen and say back what you think I'm saying."

The Dress Rehearsal. "I'll briefly tell you the situation, then I'd like one of you to be the other person. I'll practice what I'm planning to say, then I'd like your feedback."

The Huddle. "I'd like help mapping out a step-by-step strategy or plan for doing _____."

The Brainstorm. "I'm too close and can't see the forest for the trees. Let's brainstorm all the possible and impossible things I could do regarding the situation I'll briefly describe to you."

Ann Landers. "I'll briefly tell you what's going on. Then you give me advice—tell me what you would do. I may not take your advice, but I'd like to hear what it is."

Mount Vesuvius. "I'd like to gripe and fume and blow my stack for three minutes, just to get it out of my system. (Set the timer!) Then I'll choose an option from above."

▶ Write down any agreements you make with your group, steps you'll take, or scripts you've come up with in your notebook.

▶ Set the time and place for your next meeting. Consider that a missed or postponed meeting may mean there's something you'd rather not deal with, then choose to go toward the issue rather than burying it.

▶ Do an energy check at the end of each meeting. Let each person say, "On a scale of 1 (low) to 10 (high), after this meeting I feel like a _____." Then tell why and what you need to feel good about going forward toward more career security or your new job. Thank people for their attention and advice.

Index

About the Authors

Contacts Count is the premier training company for face-to-face, business and career networking, offering a wide variety of learning opportunities in the U.S. and Canada. We (Anne Baber and Lynne Waymon) are the founders and principals. For the past seventeen years, we've helped clients realize the many strategic applications for networking and have worked with them to increase their employee and member expertise. We also are currently expanding our cadre of outstanding Certified Contacts Count Presenters.

Networking is the pivotal professional capability for today's businessperson. We recognize the commitment and practice it takes to learn the skills in this book. We want to help you put more profit, purpose, and pleasure into all of your business and career relationships.

If you are a member of an association or networking organization, pass our contact information along to the person or committee responsible for programming. Our keynotes and workshops, always rated "Outstanding," will help your members put these leading-edge networking skills to use immediately.

If you work for an organization—from a high-tech firm to a university to a defense contractor—we can help you foster a positive networking culture of inclusiveness and inquiry, both within the organization and in outside relationships. Our consulting and training services help organizations create strategic plans to build cross-functional relationships that get the job done, boost profits, and expand influence in the marketplace.

Our Products and Services

1. Presentations: Keynotes, Workshops, Training Courses, Webinars, Teleseminars ("Networking Know-How: The Contents Court System for Savvy Professionals & Smart Companies")

2. Skill-Building Materials: Books, E-books, CDs, articles for reprint, Guide (*Ten Networking Activities for Events at Associations, Alumni Groups, & Corporations*), *The Fireproof Your Career Toolkit*

3. Coaching and Consulting for individuals and organizations

4. In-house Train-the-Trainer Programs to certify employees to deliver our programs internally

5. In-house Licensure, allowing organizations to use our copyrighted materials

6. Training for individuals who wish to become Certified Presenters

Our Corporate, Government and Association Experience

▶ Leadership Programs for Fortune 500 Companies

▶ Special Interest and Affinity Group Workshops at Fortune 500 Companies

▶ Skill-Building Training for Non-Profits, Corporations, and Associations.

▶ Keynotes and Workshops at Professional Association Conferences

▶ Career/Management Development Programs for Corporations, Government Agencies, and Associations

▶ Training for Universities, MBA Programs, Government Agencies, Corporations, Keynotes and Workshops for Alumni Groups, Chambers of Commerce, Business Expos

▶ Webinars and Tele-seminars for Associations, Corporations, and Career Development Firms

Recent Clients

Lockheed Martin; Deloitte Financial Advisory Services; National Geographic Society; Georgetown University; Marquette University; Corning, Inc.; U.S. Departments of State, Commerce, Agriculture, Navy; BoozAllen; National Association of Home Builders; American Council of Engineering Companies; Public Relations Society of America; Tri-State Women Entrepreneur's Expo; National Association of Female Executives; Medical Librarians Association; Bank of America; Dupont, Inc.; First Horizon Bank; Heery, Inc.

Our Websites

www.ContactsCount.com
   Visit and sign up for our free Contacts Count e-newsletter.
www.FireProofYourCareer.com

Our Contact Information

Anne Baber
13433 W. 80th Terrace
Lenexa, KS 66215
Phone: 1-913-492-6873
E-mail: ABaber@ContactsCount.com

Lynne Waymon
1400 East West Hwy., Suite 1228
Silver Spring, MD 20910
Phone: 1-301-589-8633
FAX: 1-301-589-8639
E-mail: LWaymon@ContactsCount.com